# Hemingway

DONALD F. BOUCHARD

# Hemingway

SO FAR FROM SIMPLE

 **Prometheus Books**
59 John Glenn Drive
Amherst, New York 14228–2119

Published 2010 by Prometheus Books

Inquiries should be addressed to
Prometheus Books
59 John Glenn Drive
Amherst, New York 14228–2119
VOICE: 716–691–0133
FAX: 716–691–0137
WWW.PROMETHEUSBOOKS.COM

14  13  12  11  10      5  4  3  2  1

Library of Congress Cataloging-in-Publication Data

Bouchard, Donald F.
    Hemingway : so far from simple / by Donald F. Bouchard.
        p.  cm.
    Includes bibliographical references and index.
    ISBN 978–1–59102–756–0 (pbk. : alk. paper)
    1. Hemingway, Ernest, 1899–1961—Criticism and interpretation.
2. Hemingway, Ernest, 1899–1961—Literary style. I. Title.

PS3515.E37Z582535 2010
813'.52—dc22

                                                      2010003610

Printed in the United States of America on acid-free paper

To the very best grandchildren, bar none,

Zachary
Caitlyn
Jessica
Scott

It's always the same problem: that is, the relations between the subject, the truth, and the constitution of experience.

*An Aesthetics of Existence*, Michel Foucault

There is no great artist who does not make us say: "The same and yet different." (III, 259)

*Proust & Signs*, Gilles Deleuze

# Contents

# PART THREE.  "NOW THERE IS POLITICS TOO"

# CONCLUSION

# A Note on the Texts

*A*ll references to Hemingway's stories are from *The Short Stories of Ernest Hemingway*; page references in the text are from this edition. The following abbreviations for some of Hemingway's other cited works are used accordingly:

| | | |
|---|---|---|
| DIA | — | *Death in the Afternoon* |
| GHA | — | *Green Hills of Africa* |
| L | — | *Selected Letters* |
| MF | — | *A Moveable Feast* |

# Preface

*I* like a remark of Hemingway's in 1940 to Charles Scribner: "All I can do that geniuses do is not get a haircut. But finally I always have to get a haircut too." He had finished writing *For Whom the Bell Tolls* and had yet to decide on a title. His Spanish novel was in many ways a culmination of his obsession as a writer, yet his sense of himself remained derisive and ironic. He may have been exhausted: "Charlie there is no future in anything. I hope you agree. That is why I like it at war. Every day and every night there is a strong possibility that you will get killed and not have to write. I have to write to be happy whether I get paid for it or not. But it is a hell of a disease to be born with. I like to do it. Which is even worse. That makes it from a disease into a vice. Then I want to do it better than anybody has ever done it which makes it into an obsession. An obsession is terrible." I like, too, the sly movement from disease to vice to obsession, which, of course, "is terrible" but accurate nevertheless.

Describing the way he wrote his stories in *Writers at Work: The Paris Review Interviews*, he remembers, "sometimes the movement is so slow it does not seem to be moving. But there is always change and always movement." The story process and the life's career have much in common; and it will be the purpose of this study to understand that connection. "Sometimes you make it up as you go along," says Hemingway in his interview, "and have no idea how it will come out. Everything changes as it moves. That is what makes the movement which makes the story." Change is unforeseeable and often hinges on the smallest things, and, thus, the basis of his beginnings and what we might call, for lack of a better word, the "development" of his career. Hemingway started from the simplest things, both in subject matter and in manner of writing. Derisive and ironic, his beginning was lowly and, remarkably, "everything changes as it moves." So that out of his initial preoccupations, the crudity of language, and so forth, he found the basis for a genuine artistic production that engaged the decisive issues of his time.

My main emphasis is a reevaluation of the first two decades of Hemingway's activity as a writer. Additionally, I will, more briefly, examine the two works published after WWII, as they mark the end of his career. As a general approach, I have found useful the form of attention (not reading or interpretation) suggested by the works of Michel Foucault, Gilles Deleuze, and, with respect to Hemingway's career, Edward Said's *Beginnings: Intention and Method*. The costliness of form and its distinctive materiality, as it derives from specific contexts, rules, and struggles, is one of the things to be learned from these authors, and this perspective seems wonderfully suited to a writer of Hemingway's temperament. I have also made use of the published *Selected Letters*, insofar as they indicate intentions and changes on his part that are not always transparent in his writing. My purpose, however, is not biographical, although I am interested in the gains and losses, at the level of Hemingway's commitment, that a work might stand for: how, for example, the critical reception of *Death in the Afternoon* affected him and conditioned subsequent publications. These factors, found in his correspondence, are important in judging the effectiveness of a work and, finally, Hemingway's cumulative strategy. Effectiveness and a particular kind of practicality were crucial considerations for Hemingway; it extended to his dealings with Scribner's, his involvement in the minute details of the publishing business, and his refusal to engage a literary agent in his dealings with magazines. Equally, effectiveness meant the capacity to move a reader or to apply "shocks" to the system, to be memorable.

There has been any number of good and plausible "readings" of Hemingway. But it is as obvious that Hemingway has not been the object of the sort of institutionalization that has been the fate of T. S. Eliot and James Joyce or, to a lesser degree, William Faulkner. What we have seen, rather, is the spectacle of "Mr. Papa and the Parricides," the not-so-whimsical title of Malcolm Cowley's essay in *And I Worked at the Writer's Trade*. Perhaps the time is right to look again at Hemingway—not to institutionalize but to see what it is in Hemingway that resists the institution and how an attention to his works serves to establish other traditions than those that have held our attention for so long. If he saw fit to finally get a haircut, should we not at least repay his conciliatory act with a modest attention?

A personal note. In the fall of last year, my wife and I visited the Hemingway house in Key West, where a very efficient guide summed up Hemingway's career by saying that he was a drunk who kept some fifty-plus cats and lived off his wife's money. Anyhow, I got home and started thinking about a half-finished manuscript that I never seemed to get back to, so that what follows is "kinda-like" my polite response to the efficient guides who populate a writer's world.

# Acknowledgments

My interest in Hemingway began at McGill University, while team-teaching a Fitzgerald/Hemingway course with Peter Ohlin. The collegial environment of McGill and discussions with colleagues encouraged me to pursue a book-length study. I am appreciative of the support I received and for the Faculty Grant that allowed me the leisure to produce an initial manuscript. In the late stages of this project, I had the good fortune to meet Gary Scharnhorst and Robert Fleming at the University of New Mexico; they greatly helped my understanding of current Hemingway criticism. Closer to home, I am thankful to Lynette and Lee Nisbet who, more recently, prodded me to rethink an incomplete project that they felt had merit. The folks at Prometheus Books have my appreciation for the help they gave me, especially Mark Hall, Cate Roberts-Abel, and Joe Gramlich. As a source of support and good spirits, I am grateful to my lovely daughters, Nickay Manning and Alessandra Calhoun, and their husbands, Bill and Kenny, without whom, of course, there would be no dedication to this book.

My wife, Bebeann, took on the burden of retyping the original manuscript, as a further incentive to getting back to Hemingway. She has also been my principal reader, advisor, and singular support in the last few months of manuscript revisions. She has sustained my efforts with understanding and almost invariable good cheer, and I am deeply grateful.

# Introduction

*The translator talked excitedly of a dozen things sharing thoughts he had not been able to share while descending, alone at his desk, into the luminous abysses and profound crudités of American literature. "With Hemingway, the difficulty of translation—and I speak to an extent of Anderson also—is to prevent the simplicity from seeming simple-minded. For we do not have here such a tradition of belle-lettrist fancifulness against which the style of Hemingway was a rebel. Do you follow the difficulty?"*

*"Yes. How did you get around it?"*

*Petrescu did not seem to understand.*

*"Get around, how? Circumvent?"*

*"How did you translate the simple language without seeming simple-minded?"*

*"Oh. By being extremely subtle."*

*"Oh. I should tell you, some people in my country think Hemingway was simple-minded. It is actively debated."*

Updike, Beck: A Book

1

*M*y objective is reasonably straightforward. I wish to show that Hemingway was a serious writer and that his simplicity—if in fact that adequately describes his life's work, his style, and his experiments with narrative form—was the conscious product of a complex and evolving practice. *A Moveable Feast* and *Death in the Afternoon* clearly establish Hemingway's immersion in the dominant artistic movements of his time, whether in his analysis of modernism or his understanding of its decadent tendencies, not to mention his familiarity with a great number of literary modernists. *In Our Time* equally outlines his perspective with respect to his present, his specific orientation to his present circumstances, and the world he came to know. Either at the beginning or the end of his career, the same perspective exists and the same attention to his present reality. Adding to the relevance of Hemingway's response to a changing present are the changes undergone in his career over time. As a serious writer, considerations of career were inescapable, and we find ample evidence of this preoccupation in his letters. A single law applies over a long career—repetition and innovation—and it is its wavering trajectory that I intend to trace over the course of his career. Always, it is a matter of circumstances, as found, and the seriousness of his obsession with writing. The career begins simply, the outcome in part of natural talent, established conceptions of contemporary writing and art forms, and personal experience, and it gains in complexity. "*Il faut durer*," writes Hemingway, and artistic endurance is central to his achievement of a career over four decades.

It might be well to recall, however, Hemingway's reservations concerning his "afterlife," as he had observed in the career of fellow writers whose careers had ended. Writing to Arthur Mizener in response to his request for assistance with *The Far Side of Paradise*, his Fitzgerald biography, Hemingway observed: "You picked a tough subject to write about in Scott and I feel that I have let you down because I don't have his letters." He further explains:

> I remember Ford telling me that a man should always write a letter thinking of how it would read to posterity. This made such a bad

impression on me that I burned every letter in the flat includeing [*sic*] Ford's.

They should be written, he says, "not for posterity but for the day and the hour and posterity will always look after herself." He continues:

Lately I am lonely quite a lot, not haveing [*sic*] the children around and not likeing [*sic*] the way things go so that picking up the paper is like (we'll skip it). Anyway I write because it is fun to get letters back. But not for posterity. What the hell is posterity anyway? It sounds as though you were an ass. (*L*, p. 695)

Posterity, in turn and some might say justifiably, has been often critical of Hemingway. Less than a month after his assessment of the writer's relationship to his afterlife and his rejection of writers who self-consciously set the stage of their future reputations (and again to Mizener), he writes: "I think the way we are is how the world has been and these psychoanalytic versions or interpretations are far from accurate. About posterity: I only think about writing truly. Posterity can take care of herself or fuck herself" (*L*, p. 698). Hemingway had seen the working of posterity, its penchant for linking a life to a work in the absence of evidence or a "true" correspondence, in the "versions" of Edmund Wilson and Maxwell Geismar who had penetrated his defenses to reveal his psychoanalytic "wound."[1] He saw what happened, *a posteriori*, with Fitzgerald's reputation and parodied the process: "John O'Hara's introduction to *The Potable Fitzgerald* was wrapped in O'Hara's old coonskin coat that he never wore to Yale" (*L*, p. 657).

From the spectacle of reputations made and unmade, two cautionary notes: "the way we are is how the world has been" and "I only think about writing truly." There is no question that Hemingway cared about how he might be perceived after his death but only insofar as his posterity is measured by an act, "writing truly." The remainder is pathos, as he writes to Archibald MacLeish: "we'll all be gt men when we're dead and well *travaillezed* by the *ver* (worm). I hope youze know your Baudelaire: *Les morts, les pauvres morts on de grandes douleurs*" (*L*, p. 338). As another note of caution, "writing truly" should not be confused with an inflated, omnitemporal view of writing: "Scott took **Literature** so solemnly. He never understood that it was just writing as well as you can and finishing what you start" (*L*, p. 694). Hemingway engages an issue that involves more than Fitzgerald's alleged impotence after the success of *The Great Gatsby*. His pragmatism emphasizes that a romanticized notion of literature is, itself, a product of circumstances. Made into an ideal quest, literature becomes an alibi, at a more personal level, for the absence of a work.

"How the world has been" covers considerable ground, from Hemingway's involvement in two wars and the Spanish cause to his discovery of Europe, especially France and Spain. Later on, he would find Africa and Cuba and their quite disparate worlds. What he found was a world changed or quickly changing and he reflected on these occurrences: "a continent ages quickly once we come . . . but we don't know what the next changes are. I suppose they all end up like Mongolia" (*GHA*, pp. 284-85). Transformations can be observed in social relationships, family organization, and political alignments. New phenomena of Hemingway's time include as well the ongoing colonization of the oldest continents, technological advances and mechanization. None of these transformations are viewed in a positive light. Changes are both small and large: for Santiago, traditional fishing skiffs have been replaced by powerboats; a new "doom" is introduced in the Spanish civil war by fascist aviation. Identities are confused and unstable. Who truly supports the Spanish cause? Is it Loyalists, Anarchists, Republicans, Communists, Trotskyites? Even traditional practices are difficult to decipher. Who is the better bullfighter, Belmonte or Joselito?

"How the world has been" inevitably involves a perception of one's present, always with an eye toward present circumstances: "Republicans are all respectable and Pamplona is changed, of course, but not as much as we are older. I found that if you took a drink that it got very much the same as it was always. I know that things change now and I do not care. It's all been changed for me. Let it all change" (*DIA*, p. 278). As a manifesto of the work to be done in periods of change, *Death in the Afternoon* does not reveal an indifference on Hemingway's part. Rather, it presents an opportunity, an opening, in the recognition that change is not unique to his situation in time and that it need not be an obstacle to the renewal of work. Michel Fou-

important point is that his writing is interdependent of other works in "a new and substantial relationship" of writing with itself. In the same context, Foucault writes: "Flaubert is to the library what Manet is to the museum. They both produced works in a self-conscious relationship to earlier paintings and texts—or rather to the aspect in painting and writing that remains indefinitely open." And this in a period perceived as decadent: "They were not meant to foster the lamentations—the lost youth, the absence of vigor, and the decline of inventiveness—through which we reproach our Alexandrian age, but to unearth an essential aspect of our culture: every painting now belongs within the squared and massive surface of painting and all literary works are confined to the indefinite murmur of writing. Flaubert and Manet are responsible for the existence of books and paintings within works of art."[5] That the sources of the work are now to be found in the work itself has become an irrefutable aspect of the modern work of art. Some of its implications, i.e., Hemingway's particular modern style of self-reflexiveness, will be traced in the opening chapters of this study. For now, we need simply indicate its importance to Hemingway's formative, apprentice impulse. (The posthumous novels with their focus on the sources of creativity offer not a new departure for Hemingway but a recovery of the initial and formative experience of modernism. They are works of late career and are interesting for that reason, as a senescent return.) Let us emphasize, however, that the relationship of the modern writer to the "library" is tied to the aspect in modern art "that remains indefinitely open."

Turning back to the question of Hemingway's simplicity as posed by Updike, it seems plain that Hemingway's works, at the level of authorial intention, contest the "easy score"—the summary statement, the generalized word or concept—that stands for unexamined presuppositions. The mental debate with himself that follows his discussion of decadence with Gertrude Stein could not be more telling: "That night walking home I thought about the boy in the garage and if he had ever hauled one of those vehicles when they were converted to ambulances. I remembered how they used to burn their brakes going down the mountain roads with a full load of wounded . . . I thought of Miss Stein and Sherwood Anderson and egotism and mental laziness versus discipline and I thought who is calling who a lost generation" (*MF*, p. 30). Erudition and attention to particularizing detail are of consequence in disputing the charge of "simple-mindedness." *Death in the Afternoon* is explicit on the knowledge needed for "good" and effective writing. In response to Aldous Huxley's attack in "Foreheads Villainous Low," Hemingway presents his well-known definition of modern writing: "Prose is architecture, not interior decoration, and the Baroque is over." He then adds: "A good writer should know as near everything as possible. Naturally he will not. A great enough writer seems to be born with knowledge. But really is not; he has only been born with the ability to learn in a quicker ratio to the passage of time than other men and without conscious application, and with an intelligence to accept or reject what is already presented as knowledge. There are some things which cannot be learned quickly, and time, which is all we have, must be paid heavily for their acquiring. They are the very simplest things and because it takes a man's life to know them the little new that each man gets from life is very costly and the only heritage he has to leave." Hemingway goes on to explain the similarity of his position in the equally well-known passage on "the dignity of movement of an iceberg" and concludes: "And this too remember: a serious writer is not to be confounded with a solemn writer. A serious writer may be a hawk or a buzzard or even a popinjay, but a solemn writer is always a bloody owl" (pp. 190–92).

A last anecdotal remark concerning Hemingway's simplicity. In the decadent phase of the bullfight—that is, Hemingway's present— the spectacle has turned back on itself. What had been a minor means to an end, the "moment of truth," had become an end in itself. Belmonte is the key figure of this modernist reversal, "the decadent, the impossible, the almost depraved style." Joselito competed with Belmonte, the initiator of the new style, and the latter's advances were "grafted and grown into the great healthy, intuitive genius of Joselito." A golden age of the bullfight ensued, "in spite of the fact that it was in the process of being destroyed" (p. 69). In a seemingly unrelated context, Hemingway described "Up in Michigan" as his discovery of his first naturalness, a story about sexual desire about which there will be further discussion in the next chapter. The point here, however, concerns Hemingway's simplicity and the fact that a simple story of seduction in the backwoods of Michigan involves basic lessons about modernist practice, simplicity masking complexity. In a similar fashion, Joselito's "healthy" style carries with it the "the impossible, the almost depraved style" of Belmonte. It is important to realize that in speaking of Hemingway's imprecated complexity in a simple story that it not be seen as an invitation to deep interpretation. In other words, and insofar as a deep reading suggests uncovering the psychoanalytic roots of a work, a complex understanding of Hemingway's works relates to "how the world has been" and how circumstances, as he found them and as he understood them, shaped his output. What Joselito, a credible model, finds are modern, decadent conditions exemplified by Belmonte, as an existing and compelling practice. What he adds to this, what is "very costly and the only heritage that he has to leave," is a further transformation and creation, with a certain simplicity the result. How then does this clarify Hemingway's constant concern with "writing truly"? In "Miss Stein Instructs," Hemingway recalls a basic law of his distinctive literary production: "Up in that room I decided that I would write one story about each thing that I knew about. I was trying to do this all the time I was writing, and it was good and severe discipline." (*MF*, pp. 12–13)—a simple statement not without a severe discipline.

## 2

Perhaps all books, in some fashion or other, are written against other books. In a literary context, we can observe Proust writing against Sainte-Beuve and at a later stage writing against his earlier self, that being the nature of apprenticeship and future growth. With regard to Hemingway's "establishment," it is my belief that it has been far too hermetic and self-involved. Theories abound but almost always they involve some variant of the "author and his works," interpretation laced with biographical background. This critical tendency was registered by Hemingway in his lifetime and he objected to its baneful effect in obstructing his future output. With regard to feminist interpretations and other "advanced" readings, they do little good if their purpose is to prove Hemingway's misogyny, anti-semitism, or negative attitude toward gays, however much one might debate the accuracy of such charges. These remarks should not be taken as an indication that my intention is polemical. Rather, I wish to propose a wider context and another perspective on literary modernism that helps clarify Hemingway's achievements, that resonates when set side-by-side with his individual works. Far too many critics have sat in judgment of Hemingway; this one works, this one doesn't; this work is a falling off from the one that came before, he's repeating himself, or, finally, after a bad showing, welcome back Hemingway (footnotes not required). It may be more useful to understand what he was doing at a given time, why he chose one direction as against another. Beyond the earlier discussion of self-reflexiveness in his earliest writing, there is still the need to recognize that Hemingway was keenly attentive to what he was doing, self-conscious concerning the nature of his works and their significance when seen as sequential experiments—taken together as his always open text and a record of his career. It is the unraveling of these thoughts that I intend to trace, how circumstances changed and how he adapted. The perspective that I have found useful in this regard includes the early literary studies of Michel Foucault—a focus that, admittedly, he rejected in the 1970s—given that it represents a heightened awareness of the seriousness of modern literary activity. Foucault's analysis of the "limit-experience" and his ongoing analysis of knowledge and power relations, which replaced his earlier literary emphasis, also allow a reevaluation of Hemingway's allegedly naïve position on politics in the late 1930s.[6] Gilles Deleuze, a colleague of Foucault's over many years, supplies an equally provocative framework for understanding Hemingway. Deleuze introduced two ideas that situate modern literature in a distinctive fashion. The first concerns his concept of "embodied thought," that is, "the basic relations through which it is possible to think about the world;"[7] the second found in his book on Kafka (written with Félix Guattari), considers the modern literary work as deprived of a classical "access to a central viewpoint from which to represent the moral, cultural, and political structures of a society" and, consequently, forced to view society from "an oblique and marginal angle."[8] The relevance of Deleuze and Guattari's position resides in the fact that traditional, realist narrative forms, that at one time could fully represent society and were based on the belief in the effectiveness of representation as fundamental to artistic activity, have lost their hold on the modern artist. In their place are found new modes of modernist articulation, with the emphasis now on creating scenes of emotional intensity. Foucault and Deleuze are less a framework for this study or the source of an encompassing theory than guideposts for the modernist period in which Hemingway participated.

Lastly, in suggesting basic principles for understanding Hemingway's career, I have found useful the argument developed in *Beginnings: Intention and Method* by Edward Said. Two central chapters of the book deal with the nature of the modern text, as an evolving, open-ended production, and career, as a writer's attention to this central reality of his life. Said's canvas is extremely broad, covering major novelistic works from the nineteenth century through the early twentieth century. Of particular interest in Said's discussion of a modern writing career is his understanding of Foucault's importance to literary studies, especially in works such as *The Archaeology of Knowledge* and its analysis of discourse—its materiality, its constraints, its rarity and affirmation.[9] Career, examined in the light of this concept, can be traced and understood. In Hemingway's case, we can begin to appreciate, as an example, late works like *Across the River and Into the Trees* (and not be simply dismissive) or *The Old Man and the Sea* as arising from a certain stage of an evolving career and as a "statement"—rarity and affirmation, both costly and effective—made possible by his individualistic discourse (which is his text).

It may appear to some readers that I have a theory (Oh no, not more of that French stuff!); they would be incorrect. In actuality, I have many theories. While recognizing that Foucault's thought has wide application to our current thought and situation in the humanities,[10] in this instance, I favor his modest understanding of the relationship of theory and practice and on the nature of practical criticism. Foucault and Deleuze agree on the following precept concerning theory: "A theory is exactly like a box of tools. . . . It must be useful. It must function. . . . It is strange that it was Proust, an author thought to be a pure intellectual, who said it so clearly: treat my book as a pair of glasses directed to the outside; if they don't suit you, find another pair."[11] In 1980, Foucault gave an interview to *Le Monde* in which he said: "It's amazing how people like judging. Judgment is being passed everywhere, all the time. Perhaps it is the simplest thing mankind has been given to do . . . I can't help but dream about a kind of criticism that would not try to judge, but to bring an oeuvre, a book, a sentence, an idea to life; it would light fires . . ."[12]

In this short book, I have followed Hemingway's works in their chronology, with added emphasis on some more than others. The working principle, not always followed, was a more detailed treatment of those books that in my view have been ignored or those from my perspective that can be useful in better appreciating Hemingway's objectives. No single line of thought runs through the separate chapters as, I believe, no single trajectory runs through Hemingway's works, except perhaps the preoccupation of career, his experiments with literary forms, and his reflection on the changing times in which he found himself. Rather, I try to bring to bear a distinctive viewpoint in each chapter, while maintaining a degree of continuity based on "how the world has been" and changing circumstances, though not necessarily a context of progress. The criterion is effectiveness, "bringing an idea to life." A brief summary begins with the obvious recognition of the period of apprenticeship, the Paris years on through *A Farewell to Arms*, followed by a longer period of innovation, Key West and the initial movement to Cuba. The first part of this book focuses on Hemingway's "Emergence," his ambivalent modernist roots. The second and third parts examine that heterology of texts published in the 1930s. In this period, I argue, Hemingway transformed his writing and point of view from its initial modernist idiom to one more socially involved and, finally, more political. It is my purpose to show that *For Whom the Bell Tolls* sums up Hemingway's artistic development in containing and bracketing his modernist impulse within a broader view of political activity, one that does not adhere to slogans and political parties but derives from an education involving complex human relations and power struggles. As significant, the 1930s is a stage of the "Descent of Writing," which has two interrelated meanings. It is descent to those elements and circumstances that determine the functioning of institutions, but that like "this silliness of kudu" in *Green Hills of Africa* are thought of no consequence. Equally, "descent" underscores Hemingway's interest in unexamined traditions and the seemingly negligible development that shapes a *different* history. Simply stated, he examines those elements of the past, including unexamined presuppositions, that continue to affect those aspects of the present that we take for granted. Typical questions might be: Why, in the modern bullfight, is the individual given such emphasis or why Pilar's story in *For Whom the Bell Tolls* is said to carry such weight? The purpose of bringing to light this marginal history is to identify and arrest possibly negative tendencies and to open the present to the possibility of change, without any predetermination of the direction that change might take. "Let it all change," writes Hemingway in the epilogue to *Death in the Afternoon*. In the conclusion, I discuss Hemingway's last two published novels (or is it novel and novella?), where one was badly received by critics and the other gained Hemingway wide acclaim in addition to the Nobel Prize. These works I see as distillations of late career, partly myth and demystifications, the recovery of essential beliefs and self-parody, but always, as with any Hemingway work, experiments in formal innovation. In the letter, mentioned earlier, to Arthur Mizener in which Hemingway talks about Fitzgerald, he mentions the basic advice he had given: "*D'abord il faut durer*" (*L*, p. 696). Given this, I would hope that a reading of Hemingway's works is in the nature of continuing his project, at once durable and worthwhile.

# Part One
# A Twenties "Emergence"

# Chapter I

# "Necessary Measures"

## Writing and the Inner Experience

*Less and less frequently do we encounter people with the ability to tell a tale properly.*

Walter Benjamin, "The Storyteller"

*There is, of course, the problem of sustenance.*

A Moveable Feast

1

During an interlude of the hunt in *Green Hills of Africa*, Hemingway coalesces his youthful writing with his experiences of war. The catalyst fusing his private obsession as writer with the major public event of his time is a reading of Tolstoy's *Sevastopol*. "It was a very young book," he writes, "and had one fine description of fighting in it, where the French take the redoubt and I thought about Tolstoy and about what a great advantage an experience of war was to a writer." In this characteristic observation, Hemingway suggests the retrospective view of his emergence from the vignettes and stories of *In Our Time* through *A Farewell to Arms*. A double objective marks Hemingway's first writing: mapping the effects of war on his generation and, simultaneously, storming the redoubt of new writing in Paris during the 1920s. In the retrospective of *Green Hills of Africa*, WWI is more than an impetus to Hemingway's activity as writer, more than the material he would "represent." It is the basis of his differentiation, even eccentricity, with respect to earlier writers and contemporaries: "It was one of the major subjects and certainly one of the hardest to write truly of and those writers who had not seen it were always very jealous and tried to make it seem unimportant, or abnormal, or a disease as a subject, while really, it was just something quite irreplaceable that they had missed" (p. 70).[1] Hemingway speaks to the issue of "rarity"[2] in this passage, the exceptional nature of his writing and experience and the "statements," highly individualistic in their formation, that constitute his difference. It also points to the importance that Hemingway gives to his specific development and the "progress" already made in his career. In short, the experience of war is a hard-gained differentiation and the basis of the cultural significance of his works.

Throughout Hemingway's first decade as a writer, the experience of war was inescapable, as specific subject or as the general horizon encapsulating domestic scenes. Part of the achievement of *A Farewell to Arms* was in allowing Hemingway to end the apprenticeship that originated in his reaction to WWI and to begin a new phase of his career. In any event, his first war was decidedly perplexing and its effect not easily overcome, because it stood for the general collapse of individual values that overshadowed particular national defeats. It was the individual and the value of individual experience that most suffered the brutalizing effects of war. It was the individual who returned from the battlefield poorer in experience, incapable of telling his story because personal experience was now literally unaccountable, without meaning. Impersonal forces, tactical decisions, and chance events canceled individual initiative, and to recount this story was to tell a tale that was incomprehensible. Thus, the basis of a pointless vignette of *In Our Time*: "We'd jammed an absolutely perfect barricade across the bridge. . . . It was absolutely topping. They tried to get over it, and we potted them from forty yards. They rushed it, and officers came out alone and worked on it. It was an absolutely perfect obstacle. Their officers were very fine. We were frightfully put out when we heard the flank had gone, and we had to fall back" (p.

113). Measured by this scene, we can begin to appreciate Walter Benjamin's observation "that men returned from the battlefield grown silent—not richer, but poorer in communicable experience." Clearly, Benjamin shared the pathos of *In Our Time*: "A generation that had gone to school on a horse-drawn streetcar now stood under the open sky in a countryside in which nothing remained unchanged but the clouds, and beneath these clouds, in a field of destructive torrents and explosions, was the tiny, fragile human body."[3]

Another well-known vignette shows a wounded Nick Adams lying among the rubble of a war-torn village:

> "Senta Rinaldi. Senta. You and me we've made a separate peace."
> Rinaldi lay still in the sun breathing with difficulty. "Not patriots."
> Nick turned his head carefully away smiling sweatily. Rinaldi was a disappointing audience. (p. 139)

Nick's isolated condition is coterminus with his sensitivity to "the tiny, fragile human body." Further, in three of the strategically positioned stories of *In Our Time*, we encounter the isolated substance of impossible communications. The first story of the collection, "On the Quay at Smyrna," deploys the disembodied voice of a nameless officer. It introduces us to pointless wartime atrocities along with equally pointless misunderstandings among the enlisted men under his command. The shock of these experiences is inexpressible, except in the language of dreams ("That was the only time in my life I got so I dreamed about things") or bluff understatement: "It was all a pleasant business. My word yes a most pleasant business" (p. 88). "Soldier's Home," a middle story of *In Our Time*, delineates another aspect of personal loss. Recently returned from the war, Krebs finds it impossible to convey the "cool, valuable quality" he experienced at the front. His audience, he learns, was "not thrilled" by his stories. Consequently, he discovers a new value in keeping to himself, now an alien in his country, a stranger among friends and family. In the last story of *In Our Time*, we again find a soldier's return: "The story was about coming back from the war but there was no mention of the war in it" (*MF*, p. 76). Nevertheless, the effect of war is readily sensed in "Big Two Hearted River"—in Nick's self-imposed isolation, in his suppression of the past and suppression of thought, and in the skewed reality of this narrowed situation in the present. The small town of Seney, Nick first discovers, has been destroyed by fire; the accumulated experience of successive generations is flattened beyond recognition, beyond retrieval. Nick is fully alone, "a tiny, fragile human body," under the unchanging clouds of a northern Michigan sky. He has his "pack," nothing else.

"Big Two Hearted River," in particular, shows that Hemingway's interest in war extends beyond its possible use as specific subject matter. In his view, WWI dramatically altered the writer's relationship to his audience, to personal experience, to language, and to forms of writing. If "Big Two Hearted River" is the last story of *In Our Time*, it is because WWI placed a special burden on the writer, because experience and a difficult language, in the failure of ordinary language, were now inextricably linked. It might be said that the writer's exertion against a recalcitrant language reflected important aspects of a culture's identity and fate. No longer able or, perhaps, willing to identify with his culture's essential beliefs, the artist's sense of experience and the particularity of his wartime experience is only matched by images of emotional intensity. Language, then, is not the basis of normal communication and the writer no longer speaks for the dominant culture. To better understand this curious historical reversal of the artist's role, what it means to end *In Our Time* with a tense fishing story, we need to explore the background out of which "Big Two Hearted River" arose. As we shall see, this background specifically involves Hemingway's preoccupation with his writing and the experience aligned with the act of writing. For this reason, its significance as an isolated act extends to the culture at large.

2

"Big Two Hearted River" is one of two central stories of Hemingway's beginning as a writer. The other, to be discussed later, is "Up in Michigan." Both stories concern "beginning intentions."[4] They required a fundamental realignment and discovery on Hemingway's part and they continued to be replayed throughout his career. At first glance, we find an outdoor fishing scene—an idiosyncratic boy's life— and an explicit, crude seduction in a small Michigan town (with arresting dialogue). Both are primitive in the sense that they go deeper, are less changeable, more permanent than much of the Paris activity of either *The Sun Also Rises* or *A Moveable Feast* or in stories like "Cat in the Rain." Both are foundational—the visible, open air of the outdoors and the hidden, secret sexuality found in many of Hemingway's stories.

In a direct way, "Big Two Hearted River" is inaugural of Hemingway's career. According to *A Moveable Feast*, it is the first story written after the theft of his manuscripts at the Gare de Lyon. Prior to this event, Hemingway was precisely an apprentice writer, modeling his writing on Sherwood Anderson and Gertrude Stein or as a disciple of Pound, involving himself in avant-garde projects. This is a period of dependence and the establishment of artistic alliances and it is brought to a close, as Pound said, by "an act of Gawd" (*L*, p. 77n).

Hemingway had made earlier difficult choices with regard to his desire to become a writer, but now he was faced with an even more decisive question. What kind of writer would he be? His alternatives are either to write a novel or to continue "with great difficulty to write paragraphs that would be the distillation of what made a novel" (*MF*, p. 75). Although writing a novel seems a more plausible course—"it was what I should do if we were to eat regularly"—he acts out of a deeper compulsion: "What did I know best that I had not written about and lost? What did I know truly and care for the most? There was no choice at all. There was only the choice of streets to take you fastest to where you worked" (p. 76). Disillusionment has led Hemingway to his necessity and individuality as a writer and to the beginning of a "development" that would be his mainstay throughout his career. Especially early in his career, we find many instances of Hemingway's preoccupation with the nature of his text, the critical choice that begins and sustains a career. In any event, the logic underlying Hemingway's reflection is based on a "fortuitous and inevitable" event that sets aside the earlier work that was produced out of conscious volition or the "lyric facility of boyhood that was as perishable as youth was." His discovery of an essential imperative of modern writing is expressed in the simplest formulation: "There was no choice at all." What was needed was to put his suffering to work, through impressions that are "hewn out of life, delivered in a work."[5]

In an opening section of *A Moveable Feast*, Hemingway speaks of those times "when starting a new story and (he) could not get it going." Then he thinks, "Do not worry. You have always written before and you will write now. All you have to do is write one true sentence. Write the truest sentence that you know." What then is a true sentence? Is it, in the simplest sense, a true "sentence that I knew or had seen or had heard someone say" (p. 12)? If so, what makes it true? Obviously, the sentence has a relationship to contemporary reality and to his present experience. Does that relationship make the sentence true? What decisively connects an observation, however faithfully recorded, to the artist's imperative that "there was no choice at all"? As a reflection of his apprenticeship, *A Moveable Feast* suggests the kind of acuity that Gilles Deleuze finds in Proust, who underwent a similar, visible apprenticeship. Proust's "search" for truth, writes Deleuze, led him to discount the philosophical attraction of "the method." In its place, Proust introduces the double idea of "constraint" and "chance." Truth depends on an encounter, on an event that forces true thought to arise and that determines the nature of an ongoing search that is the substance of the literary text. "The accident of encounters and the pressure of constraints are Proust's two fundamental themes."[6] Given these conditions, the genuine "true sentence" has a necessity not found in volitional activity; it is found, not willed.

"Art is the apotheosis of solitude," says Beckett in his study of Proust; "the artistic tendency is not expansive, but a contraction."[7] "Big Two Hearted River" contracts the casualties of war and transplants accidents and misfortunes into the emerging outline of the writer's necessity. (In the opening passage of *A Moveable Feast*, Hemingway describes his technique for writing short stories: "That was called transplanting yourself, I thought" [*MF*, p. 5].) The story quickly subordinates an initial scene of devastation, because "the river was there. It swirled against the log piles of the bridge" (p. 209). Recalling this crucial renewal in *A Moveable Feast*, Hemingway writes:

> When I stopped writing I did not want to leave the river where I could see the trout in the pool, its surface pushing and swelling smooth against the resistance of the log-driven piles of the bridge. The story was about coming back from the war but there was no mention of the war in it.

But in the morning the river would be there and I must make it
and the country and all that would happen. There were days ahead
to be doing that each day. No other thing mattered. In my pocket
was the money from Germany so there was no problem. When that
was gone some other money would come in. All I must do now was
to stay sound and good in my head until morning when I would start
to work again. (pp. 76–77)

At the moment of greatest loss, Hemingway unexpectedly finds his
life's work and the possibility of transforming the personal experience
he "knows best" into a work, "excavated, pre-existing within the
artist, a law of his nature."[8] Hemingway has undergone a conversion—"no other thing mattered"—and it has the unshakable confidence of any new faith, "when that was gone . . ." Written in the last
years of Hemingway's life, *A Moveable Feast* is a testimony to the
career that renews beginning intentions and to the ever-continuing
text "when I would start to work again."

The experience of loss is basic to the definition of Hemingway's
"code hero." But it is important to emphasize that it is the experience
of the artist that anchors Hemingway's codified scene, perhaps most
insistently when he is nowhere to be seen. The writer deals with the
consequences of his disruptive time and, of note, he recognizes and
prizes a highly limited reality. In his Paris apprenticeship, Hemingway
observed the excesses of expatriot colleagues and friends and its effect
on their work and personal relationships. The portrait of Gertrude
Stein in *A Moveable Feast* serves as an example, and there are many
others. In each case, there is a transgression of limits and an exhaustion of talent, of work, and finally, of life. But Hemingway, as we shall
see, was also drawn to this "limit-experience" throughout his career.

In any case, resources must be husbanded in a beginning career,
rules established: "All I must do now was to stay sound and good in my
head . . ." Nick Adams, for his part, must resist the lure of the swamp:
"He felt a reaction against deep wading with the water deepening-up
under his armpits, to hook big trout in places impossible to land them"
(p. 231). Hemingway's "constraints" are self-created as a condition of
his work. The discipline of a detailed routine, described in *A Moveable
Feast*, as accompanying the writing process is not decoration.

In "Big Two Hearted River," detailed activity is set against a limited natural world. In the renewal of the story, we find a reflection of artistic reversals and adaptations that secures pleasure: "I did not want to leave the river where I could see the trout in the pool, its surface pushing and swelling against the log-driven piles of the bridge." Writing substitutes manageable rules and, as a repeated exertion against resistances, it creates a pleasurable effect of "swelling smooth." A more explicit instance of this process is found in *Death in the Afternoon*, where the importance of the second act of the bullfight is stressed as a required transformation of the bull's "free, wild quality":

> When I learned the things that can be done with him as an artistic property when he is properly slowed and still has kept his bravery and his strength I kept my admiration for him always, but felt no more sympathy for him than for a canvas or the marble a sculpture cuts or the dry powder your skis cut through. (pp. 98–99)

"Transplanting" to an artistic medium, not without its own specific dangers, is fundamental to the integrity of an ensuing action in which the artist is indistinguishable from the totality of the "work in progress." This, for Hemingway, is the strenuously achieved figure of simplicity on the basis of which "no other thing mattered."

Earl Rovit, in a thoughtful study, states that Manuel, the bullfighter in "The Undefeated," is an excellent example of a simpler man for whom "thought and action (or reaction) are simultaneous."[9] In Hemingway's language:

> His instincts and his knowledge worked automatically, and his brain worked slowly and in words. He knew all about bulls. He did not have to think about them. He just did the right thing. His eyes noted things and his body performed the necessary measures without thought. If he thought about it he would be gone.
>
> Now, facing the bull, he was conscious of many things at the same time . . . but his only thought was in words: "*Corto y derecho.*"
>
> "*Corto y derecho,*" he thought, furling the mullets. Short and straight. (p. 260)

"*Corto y derecho*" is less a thought than a part of Manuel's "necessary measures." Only the thought that arises from a practice, that returns to enable a practice, has value in the transposition to an artistic plane. And, here, rooted in Hemingway's most individualistic "necessity" as a writer, we locate an essential tenet of modernism. Conceptualization and the modern work of art are antonyms, the work being exactly that which goes beyond conceptualization and conventional thought. "If he thought about it he would be gone," and so too the work that derives from the interrelation of the artist and the work. Hemingway observes, "If I started to write elaborately, or like someone introducing something or presenting something, I found that I could cut that scrollwork or ornament out and throw it away and start with the first true declarative sentence I had written" (*MF*, p. 12). Equally, it is on this basis that Hemingway can insist on the intrinsic connection of his writing to modern painting (especially Cézanne) or, oppositely, can crudely dissociate himself from a failed writer ("Take your dirty camping mouth out of here" [p. 92]), or, can be skeptical of Fitzgerald "who did not stop talking" (p. 148), or, finally, be aware of the artistic integrity of *The Great Gatsby*, because "to hear him talk about it you would never know how very good it was, except that he had that shyness about it that all non-conceited writers have when they have done something very fine" (p. 152). "To stay sound and good in my head" means to abdicate thought and resist conceptualizations about his work, the "work"—"until morning when I would start work again," and thought could be integrated into his practice.

A different form of experience aligned with the practice of writing was Hemingway's initial goal, as his purpose was to counteract the dissociation of WWI, to locate a space, however narrowed, where an individual could recover a personal stake in practice. It is not farfetched to speak of Hemingway's ethics when we consider his discipline and his perception of writing as a certain, evolving relationship to himself. Of course, the ambiguity of Hemingway's discovery of writing is that it can only maintain the value of individual exertions through a medium that is essentially nondiscursive. A "representative" language of "common-sense" is the fundamental loss that grounds the activity of *In Our Time*.

3

Recall Nick Adams's separate peace, the fact that Rinaldi "was a poor audience"; consider the reticence that Hemingway felt to be essential to the integrity of the work of art. These factors suggest that the act of writing corresponds to an inner experience, which the writer is either unwilling to reveal or can only express through the indirection of the work of art. The inner experience reveals itself at precisely the point where thought is impotent and in a specific practice that stretches physical resources *to the limit*, a good example being Nick Adams's skiing at the beginning of "Cross-Country Snow":

> The rush and the swoop as he dropped down a deep undulation in the mountain side plucked Nick's mind out and left him only the wonderful flying, dropping sensation in his body. He rose to a slight up-run and then the snow seemed to drop out from under him as he went down, down, faster and faster in a rush down the last steep slope. Crouching so he was almost back on his skis, trying to keep the center of gravity low, the snow driving like a sand-storm, he knew the pace was too much. But he held it. He would not let go and spill. Then a patch of soft snow, left in a hollow by the wind, spilled him and he went over and over in a clashing of skis, feeling like a shot rabbit, then stuck, his legs crossed, his skis sticking up and nose and ears full of snow. (p. 183)

This is skiing as "corto y derecho," where exhilaration and an excessive movement end in collapse and exhaustion, leaving Nick "like a shot rabbit." As Michel Foucault writes in "Preface to Transgression," the inner experience arises from "the related categories of exhaustion, excess, the limit, and transgression—the strange and unyielding form of these irrecoverable movements that consume and consummate us."[10] It is the product of the "hunger" delineated throughout *A Moveable Feast* as the desire of writing and it is known through the sensationalism of *In Our Time*, a double sensationalism since, of course, the experience is provocative and excessive and since it seeks to uncover "raw" sensations.

Hemingway's characters satisfy their individual "hunger" through experiences and practices that are unproductive from a "normal" point of view. Of consequence in "Cross-Country Snow," the pregnancy of Nick's wife conditions his imminent return to the States and, one presumes, a state of productive normalcy. Foucault writes that the inner experience is opposed to the dialectic of production that has defined man as worker since the eighteenth century. Dialectic imagines a situation of present loss and future compensation and recovery. What links the two states is work. Human history, in this light, is productivity; it is "the 'work' *par excellence*," or "the triumph of meaning."[11] At the end of a long struggle, the subterranean struggle of history, "totality" and human wholeness are said to await. Surprisingly, this understanding constitutes the implicit ideology of both bourgeois and advanced Marxist thought, as a nostalgic circle of recovery. In Hemingway's "The Revolutionist," one finds Hemingway's skepticism concerning a faith in the future that awaits mankind:

> "But how is the movement going in Italy?" he asked.
> "Very badly," I said."
> "But it will go better, he said. "You have everything here. It is the one country that every one is sure of. It will be the starting point of everything." (p. 157)

The laconic tale ends: "The last I heard of him the Swiss had him in jail near Sion." Hemingway's more typical characters, on the contrary, achieve marginal definition and satisfaction only in a present state of dislocation and disorientation. They value experiences that are of the moment and that provisionally arrest the flow of time, experiences that, for this reason, are excessive and transgressive of ordinary expectations and behavior.

If the inner experience is a source of notoriety in the modernist context, as well as a basis of the modernist sublime, it is because its essential movement is tied to "the scandalous, the ugly, the impossible."[12] In Hemingway and other modernist writers, sexuality is at the core of the inner experience: prohibited, transgressive sexuality, lost-generation sex and decadent excesses, not the "connubial bliss" that forces Nick Adams to return to the States. In a broader sense, sexuality was barometric of Hemingway's early practice as a writer, the virtual code of his modernist impulse and integrative pattern of writing and the inner experience. It is no accident that Robert Cohn, who is described as experiencing writer's block in *The Sun Also Rises* and feels that "my life is going so fast and I'm not really living it" (p. 10), partially resolves his dilemma upon meeting Brett, a disorienting "sex-object." More important, however, to an understanding of the relation of eroticism to writing is *A Moveable Feast*. At the very beginning of this document of the modernist sublime that sustains Hemingway's writing, we are introduced to a scene in a café on the Place St.-Michel. The young author is at work on a story about "up in Michigan" when an attractive girl enters the café: "I looked at her and she disturbed me and made me very excited." In a crucial "transplanting," the girl is made a part of the story ("you belong to me now"):

> I entered far into the story and was lost in it . . . then the story was finished and I was very tired. I read the last paragraph and then looked up and looked for the girl and she had gone. I hoped she had gone with a good man, I thought. But I felt very sad.

More explicitly, he draws the connection between writing and eroticism: "after writing a story I was always empty and both sad and happy, as though I had made love . . ." (pp. 5–6). The same isolated individuality, the same movement sustains writing and sex. As well, the two give rise to the same feeling and end in an emptying that is "both sad and happy."

"Up in Michigan," the second of Hemingway's inaugural stories and as important to a definition of his early writing as "Big Two Hearted River," was initially published in the experimental *Three Stories and Ten Poems*. "Up in Michigan" is essential to an understanding of early Hemingway; it is the Hemingway who disciplined his writing to the point where it coincided with a basic element of modern experience. He had wanted to include it in the first commercial publication of *In Our Time*, but Boni & Liveright refused. It was the story that Gertrude Stein judged "*inaccrochable*," despite Hemingway's insistence, "what if it is dirty but it is only that you are trying to use words that people actually use" (*MF*, p. 15). Many years later, when preparing the publication of *The First Forty-Nine Stories*, he rehearsed a more elaborate argument for Maxwell Perkins:

> The book is to be a definitive collection of all the stories up to now. Without Up in Michigan it is not that. If the story is cut it loses all importance.

It is an important story in my work and one that has influenced many people. Callaghan etc. It is not dirty but very sad. I did not write so well then, especially dialogue. Much of the dialogue is very wooden in that story. But there on the dock it suddenly got absolutely right and it is the point of the whole story and the beginning of all the naturalness I ever got. (*L*, p. 468)

Hemingway's discovered "naturalness in his writing" was simultaneously the beginning of his reputation as a scandalous writer, the dissolute character who so disturbed his mother in his initial reception in America.

Undoubtedly, "Up in Michigan" is an imperfect story, but as Hemingway observes in *Death in the Afternoon*, it is best to begin with "*novillada*" productions if one "wants to learn about technique, since the employment of knowledge that we call by that bastard name is always most visible in its imperfection" (p. 17). The instruction of Gertrude Stein is visible as the story begins, in its stylistic repetition and incremental shifts in sentence structure.[13] Equally wooden are the characterizations of Liz Coates, the main character, and Jim Gilmore, the blacksmith she desires. Liz is a good person, hardworking and well liked by her employer, Mrs. Smith. The setting of the story in Horton's Bay is a good place, made up of five principal dwellings that are known by their patronymic names: a general store and post office, and, at opposite ends of the main street, a Methodist church and a township school. This orderliness, mechanically set out in Hemingway's apprentice prose, is decisive to the story's possible affect on the reader and to the fact that it "is not dirty but very sad." In a good place and among good people Liz fits in nicely, yet finds that life passes her by, which makes her fairly representative of the emotional state of numerous early Hemingway characters:

From Smith's back door Liz could see ore barges out in the lake going toward Boyne City. When she looked at them they didn't seem to be moving at all but if she went in and dried some more dishes and came out again they would be out of sight beyond the point. (p. 82)

Her one hope is Jim Gilmore. Liz "likes" Jim through all the permutations of the Steinean stutter, until "one day she found she liked it the way the hair was black on his arms and how white they were above the tanned line when he washed up in the washbasin outside the house. Liking that made her feel funny." The "funny" sensation occurs as she crosses a line. Another more decisive line is crossed when Jim is gone on a hunting trip:

> She couldn't sleep from thinking about him but she discovered it was fun to think about him too. If she let herself go it was better. The night before they were to come she didn't sleep at all, that is she didn't think she slept because it was all mixed up in a dream about not sleeping and really not sleeping. (pp. 82–83)

Now, Liz begins to cross the unutterable limit between conscious and unconscious intentions. Her composure collapses in this transgressive movement and in her "letting go." Jim, returned from deer hunting, finally responds to Liz; he comes to her as a figure of masculine violence: "then he put his arms around her. Her breasts felt plump and firm and the nipples were erect under his hands." Immediately, Liz's fear and rigidity dissolve: "She felt Jim right through the back of the chair and she couldn't stand it and then something clicked inside of her and the feeling was warmer and softer" (p. 84). Superficially, Liz is no longer the good girl we had known; she is dissolute and transgressed a moral interdiction. All of this is likely a provocation to genteel sensibility, but it is also a movement that recaptures the scene of every first time. If Hemingway's public is shocked, this indicates its resistance to transgressive experiences, the power of Hemingway's unsentimental picture of Liz insofar as her "awakening" ultimately works against her initial sentiment for Jim.

Hemingway's reading of human nature in "Up in Michigan" cannot be identified as a docile return to nature or the "serenity of anthropological truths."[14] His first "naturalness" is more nearly a denaturing of the human agent caught in the movement of eroticism. Liz is freed of her immediate surroundings and finds an undreamt disorientation, nothing approaching "a victory over self-alienation and reification."[15] The story ends with Liz silhouetted against an unnerving, natural indifference: "There as a mist coming up from the bay. She was cold and miserable and everything felt gone. . . . A cold mist was coming up through the woods from the bay" (p. 86). No judgment or moral are brought to bear; equally, eroticism leads nowhere. Liz has transgressed the taboos of Horton's Bay only to experience the return of the same limited circumstances she wanted to go beyond: "Jim stirred and curled a little tighter. Liz took off her coat and leaned over and covered him with it. She tucked it around him *neatly* and *carefully*. Then she walked across the dock and up the steep sandy road to go to bed" (emphasis added). The ending is sad, in Hemingway's view, because Liz returns to her finite existence, to her bed and her dishes on the next day. Still, it is not the end that concerns eroticism, but, rather, the reversal of the dialectic in which sex is a means to an end, bourgeois, productive sex, the "work" of making a better future. All of eroticism derives from the desire to arrest the moment when a line is crossed, from the pathological fibrillation that corresponds, at another level, to the Steinean stutter in prose:

> "Don't Jim," Liz said. Jim slid his hand further up.
> "You mustn't, Jim. You mustn't."
> Neither Jim nor Jim's big hand paid any attention to her.
> The boards were hard. Jim had her dress up and was trying to do something to her. She was frightened but she wanted it.
> She had to have it but it frightened her.
> "You mustn't do it, Jim. You mustn't."
> "I got to. I'm going to. You know we got to."
> "No we haven't, Jim. We ain't got to. Oh, it's not right. Oh, it's so big and it hurts so. You can't. Oh, Jim. Jim. Oh."
> The hemlock planks of the dock were hard and splintery and cold and Jim was heavy on her and he had hurt her. (p. 85)

A language that "says" absolutely nothing, a language that crudely flexes like orgasmic bodies, a line (of writing) that is crossed and recrossed: these are the disconcerting elements that conditioned Hemingway's early artistic exertions. When measured against the difficulties of the limit-experience, it matters little that "Up in Michigan" was thought pornographic. But it does matter that a "dirty" little story—indeed, *inaccrochable*—comes closest in the years following WWI to "performing" a new basis of individual experience. It is a gauge of Hemingway's success and that of other modern writers that the eroticism of "Up in Michigan" now seems so "natural."

Hemingway established his agenda as a writer with "Up in Michigan" and "Big Two Hearted River." His slow, painful method of writing, his not uncharacteristic "difficulty with words," stem from the movement he wanted to capture—the inner experience. Moreover, as one who wrote "about whatever (he) knew best," he knew that his "expression" in writing exposed him to the gaze of others and to an encounter of his finitude, where as speaking subject and "under each of his words, (he) is brought back to the reality of his own death."[16] Only those who deny the inner experience find composure in the speaking voice. The failure of discursive language discussed by Benjamin complements its recovery in its brute form through the inner experience.

We began this chapter with a passage from *Green Hills of Africa* that linked war with a writer's beginning intentions. Hemingway's reverie involving his youthful obsession returns with uncanny consistency to a resolution in eroticism and the inner experience that are at the heart of his writing:

> They all wanted something that I did not want and I would get it without wanting it, if I worked. To work was the only thing, it was the one thing that always made you feel good . . . so that I was happy as you are after you have been with a woman that you really love, when, empty, you feel it welling up again and there it is and you can never have it all and yet what there is, now, you can have, and you want more and more, to have, and be, and live in, to possess now again for always, for that long, sudden-ended always; making time stand still that afterwards you wait to hear it move, and it is slow in starting. (p. 72)

As a self-enclosed intensification, the limit-experience, whether found in eroticism or in writing, is intransitive. If "to work was the only thing," what does it matter if the price is the writer's repeated exposure in an act in which he is undone? This is the "limit-experience" that replays itself in Hemingway's works, that turns back on itself (intransitively) "now again for always," since the exteriority of the "always" infinite of an earlier time is no longer available.

Chapter II

# Rejecting Expatriate Practice

*The modern is acutely conscious of the contemporary scene,*
*but he does not accept its values.*
                    Stephen Spender, *The Struggle of the Modern*

*Hemingway was not a propagandist, even for humanity.*
                    Edmund Wilson

1

*H*emingway's "inaugural" impulse was self-reflexive. In this light, his posthumous novels do not represent a new direction but a confirmation or, if one prefers, a recommitment to a basic modernist orientation. In a general sense, self-reflexiveness simply points to a writing that turns back on itself for its means and materials and its constituent language. Connecting the essential modernist strands of language and experience, John Rajchman says: "the 'source' or 'essence' of art (and particularly of literature), the source that modernism finds or restlessly seeks (finds *by* restlessly seeking) is also the source or essence of experience, at least of *our* experience." An extended history subsumes the emergence of an autonomous language as the source of modern literature. One of the aspects of the artist's

49

encounter with language in itself is a loss of the classical subordination to "discourse" and the regulative functions of "good taste, pleasure, naturalness, and truth." Thus, a nondiscursive reality is discovered in the "mad" source of experience, insofar as modern writing "transcends or transgresses that which constitutes its limits." Modern writing and abstract art do something—as performance—that cannot be done in any other way and it is in this sense that they are "intransitive." They bring us to an encounter of our limits—"our own death, our object-less angst, our nameless desire, our fitful 'eroticism'"— and, for the artist in his "finitude," the limits of what can be represented.[1]

Much of *A Moveable Feast* replays Hemingway's discovery of his "necessary measures" and the twin lines of his inner experience. But it also depicts the counterpart to his modernist obsession, precisely the "figures of contempt and condemnation." Sexuality, not surprisingly, is also the basis for understanding his contemporaries and his critical attitude towards them. Hemingway did not hide his contempt for Wyndham Lewis, "the eyes had been those of an unsuccessful rapist" (p. 109). Nor was his dismissive sketch of Gertrude Stein any less brutal or sexually revealing:

> I heard someone speaking to Miss Stein as I had never heard one person speak to another; never anywhere, ever. Then Miss Stein's voice came pleading and begging, saying "Don't, pussy. Don't. Don't, please don't. I'll do anything, pussy, but please don't do it. Please don't. Please don't pussy." (p. 116)

Then there is Hemingway's complicated relationship with Fitzgerald:

> "Zelda says that the way I was built I could never make any woman happy and that was what upset her originally. She said it was a matter of measurements. I have never felt the same since she said that and I have to know truly."
> "Come out to the office," I said.
> "Where is the office?"
> "*Le water*," I said. (p. 188)

Sexual unmanning is identified as the betrayal of talent. Hemingway's sketches are not entirely one-sided; at the end of *A Moveable Feast*, we find a description of his disloyalty as husband and writer.

From the beginning of his "necessity" as writer, Hemingway's life and works were entwined in a spiraling relationship, as they would remain throughout his career. Paris ends, as does his first phase of productivity, when he betrays his self-imposed standards. Simultaneously, he "sells out" to the rich and abandons Hadley for Pauline Pfeiffer. Nothing remains unchanged, and, towards the end of his life, he admits his responsibility. Yet, there now exists a new, more sinister and anonymous background: the indifferent forces of a new barbarism, "who, when they had passed and taken the nourishment they needed, leave everything deader than the roots of any grass Attila's horses hooves have ever scoured" (p. 206). This description extends the contempt leveled at sexual perversions to the culture at large: "the petit bourgeois consumer of mass culture, the inauthentic *das Man* with its 'idle chatter,' the 'last man' of our flat, leveled down ascetic modern culture, the 'neurotic' whose life is a long unsuccessful denial of his perversion, anxiety, rage, and death."[2]

"Paris was never to be the same again," writes Hemingway, "although it was always Paris and you changed as it changed" (pp. 208–209). *The Sun Also Rises* records this transformation, being at once a coda to the Paris years and the self-sufficiency of Hemingway's earliest writing and a displacement of his "hunger" to Spain, where he found a new beginning and a revitalized relationship to his writing. There was as well the question of audience and the reality of Spanish *afición* that promised an audience responsive to artistic integrity. On the one hand, *The Sun Also Rises* explores the irrelevance of expatriate excesses in Paris, the impotence and pointlessness of sexual adventurism; on the other hand, something that "abideth forever"— the earth, of course, but also something we "would always have" (p. 149), in Jake's phrase, because of a redefinition of the concept of the work. Spain would provide an antidote to the reality of failed romances as well as the romantic artist that were current in Hemingway's time—in short, a new basis for the writer's exertion, no longer modeled on biological engenderment or its failure ("irony and pity") but on the bullfight. In this sense, Spain will provide a second apprenticeship, as reflected in *The Sun Also Rises*.

2

At first in the novel, there is the enigma of Robert Cohn, the novelist: "he wrote a novel, and it was not really such a bad novel as critics later called it, although it was a very poor novel" (pp. 5–6). What measure distinguishes a "bad" from a "poor" novel? What, at a later time, made it bad for critics and always "a very poor novel"? No doubt, the answer lies in the novel's topicality. In any case, Cohn is now unable to overcome a spectacular writer's block, which he blames in part on Frances, his fiancée: "You know Robert is going to get material for a new book. Aren't you Robert? He's decided that I don't film well . . . so now he's going out to get some new material . . . We all ought to make sacrifices for literature" (p. 50). We can speculate, on the basis of this remark, that Cohn had channeled his unhappy life into his first novel and that it used up his only resources as a writer. He must now repeat this parasitic process. Hemingway's satire suggests that it is preferable to sacrifice certain kinds of literature and particular stereotypes of the suffering romantic artist:

> I know the real reason why Robert won't marry me, Jake. It's just come to me. They've sent it to me in a vision in the Café Select. Isn't it mystic. Like at Lourdes. Do you want to hear, Robert? I'll tell you. It's so simple. I wonder why I never thought about it. Why, you see, Robert's always wanted to have a mistress, and if he doesn't marry me, why then, he's had one. She was his mistress for two years. You see how it is? And if he marries me, like he's always promised he would, that would be the end of the romance. (p. 51)

Harvey Stone had labeled Cohn "a case of arrested development" (p. 41), and, unfortunately, this charge appears to cover both his personal conduct and artistic orientation. He uncritically adopts what, at an earlier time, had been a productive tendency, unaware that any form contains its eventual historical falsification. Caught between Frances and Brett, Cohn is fated to live out the parody of Bill Gorton's witty invention in Burguete, when he sings "Irony and Pity" to the tune of "The Bells Are Ringing for Me and My Gal." A once sad, pointed story is emptied out as a popular song in the present. The dissonance that comes from the encounter of Gorton's new realism and an old romance is found in all of the love relationships of *The Sun Also Rises*. It is the last word struck by the novel:

> "Oh, Jake," Brett said, "we could have had such a damned good time together." . . .
>     "Yes," I said. "Isn't it pretty to think so."

Romance as pointless story, as well, underscores the unstated irony of the "wonderful story" that Jake reads in Burguete:

> I sat against the tree trunk of two of the trees that grew together, and read. The book was something by A. E. W. Mason, and I was reading a wonderful story about a man who had been frozen in the Alps and then fallen into a glacier and disappeared, and his bride was going to wait twenty-four years exactly for his body to come out on the moraine, while her true love waited too, and they were still waiting when Bill came up. "Get any?" he asked. (p. 120)

By remaining faithful to the woman's dead husband and to each other, the lovers waste their lives. In Mason's "The Crystal Trench," the husband's body is recovered punctually twenty-four years later.[3] Brought to the top of the moraine it instantly turns to dust, leaving only the locket the husband had worn. The sentimental token reveals the picture of another woman.

Flaubert had exhausted the love interest in novels in *Madame Bovary* and Hemingway uses Jake's impotence to block the elaboration of a romance story line:

> "Oh, darling," Brett said, "I'm so miserable."
>     I had a feeling of going through something that had happened before. "You were happy a minute ago."
>     The drummer shouted; "You can't two time—"
>     "It's all gone."
>     "What's the matter?"
>     "I don't know. I just feel terribly." (p. 64)

Each time Emma Bovary enacts a desire fed by her reading, she does so more crudely and with less intensity. The decay of love's narrative makes for sadly superfluous fates. The narrative of romantic love is now of so little consequence in *The Sun Also Rises* that it is displaced to the backwaters of San Sebastian, where Brett and Robert Cohn act out their second-rate plot.

*The Sun Also Rises* immunizes against what *A Moveable Feast* labels the "germ of professionalism" and it subverts the novelistic norms that gain an author a wide audience, including anything that suggests categorical perception. Morse Peckham locates in this the ethical foundation of Hemingway's works, in his defense of individuality and individual expression at the expense of the group, any group. Concerning Hemingway's break with Miss Stein, Peckham writes: "His objection to her was not that she was a lesbian. Rather, his rejection was based on his comprehension of her gradual corruption. . . . Her corruption lay simply in the fact that she moved from a defense of homosexuality to the assertion that homosexuality is a proof of superiority."[4] This development is understandable, given the likely elaboration of a defensive attitude, but in moving from defensiveness to an assertion of superiority, one denies others their right of individual preference, the original basis of Stein's claim. Jake's anger at homosexuals in *The Sun Also Rises* is accountable in these terms: "I was very angry. I know they are supposed to be amusing, and you should be tolerant, but I wanted to swing on one, any one, anything to shatter that superior, simpering composure" (p. 20). Much the same anger is directed at Cohn: "He looked a great deal as his compatriot must have looked when he saw the promised land. Cohn, of course, was much younger. But he had that look of eager, deserving expectation" (p. 22). Explicitly in Pamplona: "'That Cohn gets me,' Bill said. 'He's got this Jewish superiority so strong that he thinks the only emotion he'll get out of the fight will be being bored'" (p. 162).

More than any other character, it is Bill Gorton who sets himself against categorical thought or an individual case that tries to establish its normative status. He punctures solemnities, displays the fragility of sensible accommodations, and corrupts with ease cultural truisms or the genealogies of "simpering composure." He satirizes William Cullen Bryant by applying a "chicken-and-the-egg" routine: "We should not question. Our stay on earth is not for long. Let us rejoice and give thanks" (p. 121). He then takes on other "great" Americans:

"I had a lovely dream," Bill said. "I don't remember what it was about, but it was a lovely dream."

"I don't think I dreamt."

"You ought to dream," Bill said. "All our biggest business men have been dreamers. Look at Ford. Look at President Coolidge. Look at Rockefeller. Look at Jo Davidson." (p. 124)

The very fact of a list of dreamers is preposterous, using the favorite device of categorical thought and including an element that upsets fixed categories. Starting with Ford, who argued that the regimented eight-hour day would free workers for cultural pursuits and who wanted to make the workplace the foundation for mass acculturation, Bill concludes with Jo Davidson, a financially successful American sculptor, who had numerous commissions for monumental sculptures of American heroes and politicians. Financially motivated dreams are attacked, but so too a changed American culture rooted in a masked and more insidious form of regimentation. Opposed to dreamers, Bill Gorton is attracted to the everyday, in Vienna, the streets of Paris, in Burguete and Pamplona, anywhere something possesses intrinsic and substantial popular appeal by virtue of the long-standing appreciation of ordinary people. Since his attraction is to individual cases, his interests are heterogeneous, and involve many meanings and various pleasures. One thing they are not is epic and heroic, *à la* Jo Davidson. If we examine the behavior and characteristics of the novel's cast of characters, we can appreciate the relevance of Foucault's assertion: "the psychological dimension in our culture is the negation of epic perception."[5] This observation is especially pertinent to Jake and Brett, their subjectivity, and to the secrets and anguish they share.

Through Bill Gorton, we see Hemingway repositioning the authorial function within a wider, more complex social reality, one opposed, of necessity, to the claustrophobic Paris *avant garde* of little magazines or to New York literary fashions; and, from a psychological point of view, Bill Gorton is refreshingly unproblematic. (The next chapter examines the importance of the bullfight for Hemingway as a more critical, explicit opposition to the Paris and New York literary scene.) *A Moveable Feast* makes plain Hemingway's increasing dissatisfaction with the Paris scene and his principle tutors, Gertrude Stein and Pound. It is well known that *The Sun Also Rises* was written in part against Stein's magisterial pronouncement on his generation and *A Moveable Feast* also shows his resistance to Pound's fanciful *"Bel Esprit"* and his insistence on the *"mot juste*—the one and only correct word to use."[6] Unlike his break with Miss Stein, Hemingway retained his fondness for Pound, but he no longer believed that the "great treasure" that was Paris, "all this new world of writing," could be summed up in a single word. Hemingway had found Russian writing and it is surely meaningful that in Pamplona, Jake reads *A Sportsman's Sketches*, or that Hemingway's parody of Sherwood Anderson takes its title from Turgenief. "All this new world of writing" gave Hemingway the courage to question his tutors as their discipline slackened. Maxwell Perkins was undoubtedly correct in his initial assessment of *The Sun Also Rises*: "a healthy book, with marked satirical implications upon novels which are not—sentimentalized, subjective novels, marked by sloppy hazy thought."[7] This same impulse underlies *The Torrents of Spring*, Hemingway's satire of Sherwood Anderson.

Written between the first and final drafts of *The Sun Also Rises*, Hemingway's parody focuses precisely on Anderson's loose, subjective thought and sentimental generalities. "The best by Test" reads the billboard of Brown's Beanery, where much of the action of *The Torrents* occurs, and Hemingway tests Yogi Johnson (Anderson's pseudonym) to show the flatulence of *Dark Laughter*:

> "Forward to the beanery." Yogi spoke quietly. He was a white man, but he knew when he had had enough. After all, the white race might not always be supreme. This Moslem revolt. Unrest in the East. Trouble in the West.
>
> Things looked black in the South. Now this condition of things in the North. Where was it taking him? Where did it all lead? Would it help him to have a woman? Would spring ever come? Was it worthwhile after all? He wondered. (p. 74)

Generally, critics have been harsh in judging Hemingway's intention and find equally difficult the handling of Stein and Pound in *A Moveable Feast*. The consensus, it seems, is that the Anderson parody, if not written out of spite or ill-will, was a crude attempt on Hemingway's part to break his contract with Boni & Liveright. Based on the letter to Horace Liveright that accompanied Hemingway's submission of *The Torrents*, this argument is unconvincing. In considerable detail, Hemingway explained his reasons for thinking his parody would be a successful publishing venture. He sets out an ambitious comparison of his situation to "the golden age of the novel," where Fielding wrote "his satirical novels as an answer to the novels of Richardson." He remarks that many of his friends were delighted with the parody and that there always exists a ready market for funny books. Admitting that it might offend Anderson, he says that no one "with any stuff can be hurt by satire." Finally, he considers in an explicit fashion the parody's long-term advantages: "it should be to your interest to differentiate between Sherwood and myself in the eyes of the public and you might as well have us both under the same roof and get it coming and going. . . . It does not depend on Anderson for its appeal, but it has that to start with. It should start plenty of rows, too. And anybody who has read a word by Anderson will feel strongly about it — one way or the other" (*L*, pp. 172–74). In a straightforward fashion, Hemingway tried to deal with the issue of literary vitality and Boni & Liveright's financial concern. Neither Gertrude Stein nor Sherwood Anderson were "figures of contempt and derision"—Hemingway had affection for both and felt understandable sadness as a result of their *contretemps*—but he wanted to be distinguished from Anderson, to be appreciated in his own right. The health of a renewed American tradition, he argued, depended on the individuality of its writers, their ability to stand by themselves, and their having the "stuff" to take it. In subsequent letters to Anderson, Hemingway addressed his perception of the subordinate status of American literature and "Great American Writers i.e., apprentice allowance claimed" (*L*, p. 206). It is clear that Hemingway wished to impose a new direction, not one that clumps writers together, but that forces them to participate in a new game, or that subjects them, through satire, to secondary rules. As he describes "the great artist" in *Death in the Afternoon*, the manner requires taking exception to the rules as they exist at his time, going beyond what "has been discovered or known about his art up to that point" (p. 100).

The fractious nature of *The Sun Also Rises* is knowable, then, as the ground and precondition for the productive emergence of art in the present. For all that, the new is unforeseeable, since it depends on individual talent: "The individual, the great artist when he comes, uses everything that has been discovered or known about his art up to that point, being able to accept or reject in a time so short it seems that the knowledge was born with him" (*DIA*, p. 100). The first indication of productive emergence is the presence of Romero at the end of the novel. Romero emerges during a period of decadence and upsets Belmonte, who had returned to the ring from retirement "to compete with Marcial, knowing it was a competition gained in advance" (p. 215). And the crowd notes their difference. Through Romero, Hemingway sets out the values he sought in the world of writing, both the expression of individual integrity and integrated action: "smoothly, calmly, and beautifully." But, as importantly, Romero's courage and grace are part of a larger world where an individual performance is valued and where honor "is as real a thing as water, wine or olive oil" (*DIA*, p. 92). "Tell him I'm ashamed of being a writer" (p. 175), Bill Gorton admits, but he could as easily have admitted his shame at being an American writer, since he is denied the intelligent interest of a native audience which prefers "genteel writing." Moreover, central to the comparison of art forms and their respective national settings is the fact that Spanish "common sense" stipulates that its "philosophy of life" be directly experienced in a practice, while American writing is seen by Hemingway as expatriated practice, increasingly fragile, extreme, and disembodied from its cultural roots. *The Purple Land* is dismissed by Jake as an example of American popular taste: "For a man to take it at thirty-four as a guide book to what life holds is about as safe as it would be to enter Wall Street from a French convent, equipped with a complete set of the more practical Alger books" (p. 9). A young nation might understandably prefer escapist literature, but it needs more to achieve maturity—a tougher, more recalcitrant, more stubbornly practical writing.

As a satire, much of *The Sun Also Rises* is concerned with the task of preparation, clearing a space for a more productive practice. Here, the bullfight should be understood less in terms of the usual critical emphasis of its manly "code" than in its nature as a specific practice connected to Hemingway's characteristic procedure in his novel. To better appreciate this facet of the novel, we must stress that the bullfight is an ephemeral and impermanent art, the kind that "Leonardo had warned against" (*DIA*, p. 99). In this sense, bullfighting is an ana-

logue for the anecdotes out of which the novel is constructed, anecdotes being fragmentary pieces of ephemeral existence and, equally, a
form of expression formed from understatement, jokes, and the "gal-
lows humor" for which Hemingway showed a special predilection.[8]
Finally, and most decisively, an anecdote, which formerly was merely
an innocuous historical fact, has undergone elaboration as a brief,
funny account of some event, usually personal or biographical. For
this reason, it now stands for the speaker's simultaneous exposure to
his listeners and to the ephemerality of his situation. In short, it parallels in a far less charged or dangerous context a bullfighter's exposure. More than likely he was joking, yet Hemingway considered ded-
icating his novel with the following inscription:

> *TO MY SON*
> John Hadley Nicanor
> This collection of Instructive Anecdotes

> (*L*, p. 199)

What is instructive is not only a lesson on things to avoid—let us
remember that the novel outraged Hemingway's more sedate readers,
including his mother, and many contemporaries who found themselves in the book—but a knowledge of where one's opportunities lie.
An anecdote is instructive and serves where other more ponderous
methods are ineffective. Love's narrative is patently ineffective as well
as Jake's attempt to think through his dilemma: "I lay thinking and
my mind jumping around . . . I was thinking about Brett and my mind
stopped jumping around and started to go in sort of smooth waves.
Then all of a sudden I started to cry" (p. 31). Something less
unnerving, more practical, is needed. Jake, however, must wait for the
second encounter with Brett in Pamplona to find his answer. After yet
another disruptive scene in a café, he returns to his room and awakens
in the middle of the night. Again the thought of Brett intrudes, this
time while reading *A Sportsman's Sketches*. "Fine philosophies" only
compound his problems as he seeks a solution. Rather, his only
recourse lies in the eclipse of thought: "what bilge I could think up at
night." In keeping with Benjamin's observation that "a thought must
be crude to come into its own action,"[9] Jake says: "What rot, I could

hear Brett say it. What rot!" Through this eruptive language, the riddle of fine philosophies is brought to ground in everyday realities and practical necessities. Less feverishly, Jake proceeds:

> When you were with the English you got in the habit of using English expressions in your thinking. The English spoken language—the upper classes, anyway—must have fewer words than the Eskimo. Maybe Eskimo was a fine language. Say the Cherokee. I didn't know anything about Cherokees, either. The English talked with inflected phrases. One phrase to mean everything. I liked them, though. I liked the way they talked. (pp. 148–49)

Jake finds a useable language, an absolutely minimal language, seemingly effortless as used by the English upper classes, that *says* far more than the elaborateness and straining of "fine philosophies." To speak like others is to share more than linguistic mannerisms; it implies the same cultural assumptions, the same heritage. Yet, the solidarity of the English upper classes in which "one phrase to mean everything" speaks to an impossible condition, at least for Jake. It, too, is part of "what bilge." It is precisely a world he does not inhabit, though he likes the feeling of talking like the English. For Hemingway, the writer is no longer part of a world in which he can easily represents its cultural values. He is more an outsider like Joseph Conrad in the *Heart of Darkness*, who "depicts English colonialism as a hell of barbarism and cruelty" and who does so by producing "specific intensive states within the English language, liberating it from its conventional rhetorical virtues of wit, elegance and satire."[10]

Given these considerations, the most remarkable aspect of Hemingway's intention in *The Sun Also Rises* is the counterpoint of the pointless romances with moments of emotional intensity. Tied to these intensive states, as a higher dimension of the relationships and painful dialogues of the novelistic characters, is the bullfight as, itself, the model of intensive experience: "And each pass as it reached the summit gave you a sudden ache inside" (p. 220).

*The Sun Also Rises*—in spite of the fact that it is entertaining and that many consider it Hemingway's best—is a limited achievement. Much of the novel is about what the novel is not about or it depicts characters who unknowingly imitate literature and, for this reason, it stands for a critique of literary antecedents. Simply stated, it is like satires generally, a work of preparation. "Nobody but Fairies can write Masterpieces or Masterpieces consciously," Hemingway wrote to Fitzgerald, "anybody else can only write as well as they can going on the system that if this one when it's done isn't a Masterpiece maybe the next one will be" (*L*, p. 305). Refreshingly, then, Hemingway's first novel was a limited achievement.

3

In a letter written in the mid-twenties to Fitzgerald, Hemingway said:

> Like me to write you a little essay on The Importance of Subject? Well the reason you are so sore you missed the war is because it is the best subject of all. It groups the maximum of material and speeds up the action and brings out all kinds of stuff that normally you have to wait a lifetime to get. . . . A dull subject I should say would be impotence. (*L*, pp. 176–77)

The war suspends "normal" development, compresses and clarifies the "stuff" of a lifetime. Emblematic of this process is a humorous exchange, near the end of *A Farewell to Arms*, between Fredcric Henry and Count Greffi, where "youth" and "old age" are shown reacting to the war:

> "What do you think of the war really" I asked.
> "I think it is stupid."
> "Who will win it?"
> "Italy."
> "Why?"
> "They are a younger nation."
> "Do younger nations always win wars?"
> "They are apt to for a time."
> "Then what happens?"
> "They become older nations." (p. 262)

None of it makes much sense but it is funny. Conventional patterns no longer apply in *A Farewell to Arms*, especially nineteenth-century novelistic paradigms. Edward Said points to the opposition at play here: "Pip's ambitions in *Great Expectations* are modeled after traditional conventions—to rise in the world, become a gentleman, gain social position, and so forth—Isabel Archer's in *A Portrait of a Lady* are vaguer: indeed, her career is, she thinks egotistically, entirely of her own making."[11] There is the Hemingway "code hero" and certain self-imposed rules but these constraints serve the ends of self-fashioning.

Hemingway's achieved mastery in *A Farewell to Arms* coincides with his perception of the terminal nature of his culture, the exhausted purposes of the culture at large. In *Hemingway's First War*, Michael Reynolds shows, with careful scholarship, the double nature of Hemingway's achievement. According to Reynolds, Hemingway magnifies his personal experience of WWI and the undeniable shock he experienced when he was wounded as an aspect of his general indictment of the rationale for the war's failures. For this reason, Frederic Henry's desertion was "the most rational choice he makes and it becomes a radical political statement indicating the national goals that had failed to sustain the individual."[12] Hemingway studied historical documents in preparation for writing his novel and he intended an objective political analysis of cultural disintegration—in Hemingway's language a "true" record of the major catastrophe of his age. The second of Reynolds's considerations involves the novel's form and its distinctive handling of artistic resources. With respect to his subject matter, Hemingway exploited the best war novels of the European and American tradition, specifically borrowing from Stendhal's *The Charterhouse of Parma* and Crane's *Red Badge of Courage*. Equally, as a solidification of Hemingway's individual development, the novel evolves directly from his successful short stories and, in particular, two earlier ones: "A Very Short Story" from *In Our Time* and "In Another Country" from *Men Without Women*. (Hemingway considered *In Another Country* as a possible title.) Reynolds convincingly argues that the five-book structure of the novel is "simple and direct. Following the classic short story structure, each 'book' stops at the natural culmination of a piece of action."[13]

Two related observations can be made at this point. *A Farewell to Arms* follows the same pattern as *The Sun Also Rises*. An initial situation progressively exhausts itself, leaving Frederic Henry with nowhere to go at the end, much as Jake Barnes was faced with severely narrowed choices when he meets Brett in Madrid. An excessive movement and an inevitable exhaustion, based on an erotic relationship, outline Hemingway's typical experience. Love, in other words (an essential basis for understanding Hemingway's reflexive writing), "is a word that fills with meaning as a bladder with air and the meaning goes out of it as quickly" (*DIA*, p. 122). The doctor consoling Frederic Henry addresses a related failure of language: "I know there is nothing to say. I cannot tell you ———" (p. 331). For Hemingway at this stage of his career, the short story expresses best his core experiences, being, as it were, "natural" to them. The second observation concerns Hemingway's bending of the novel form to his purpose, as he had done through the satiric devices of *The Sun Also Rises*. Hemingway had written Perkins in the spring of 1925: "I don't care about writing a novel and I like to write short stories. . . . Somehow the novel seems to me an awfully artificial and worked out form" (*L*, p. 156). He observed that his livelihood depended on writing a novel; and he managed, in both *The Sun Also Rises* and *A Farewell to Arms*, to write what "I like to write" and to have his short stories accepted as being successful novels. Having it both ways is in the nature of Hemingway's experimentation in these novels. The intention in either case is a serious one: a critique, on the one hand, of the behavior of expatriates and their preoccupations and, on the other hand, "a critique of the primary moral systems articulated in its time."[14]

*A Farewell to Arms* rounded off Hemingway's first productive phase. It resulted from the progressive education of a decade and from a series of works marked by displacement and further solidification. It is quite literally Hemingway's farewell to the formative influence of European culture and the nihilistic tendencies that leave a disoriented Frederic Henry at the end of the novel. Hemingway's war novel tells of Americans "in another country"; and, though we are never entirely certain why Frederic Henry is in Italy, his reasons for leaving Europe resound throughout the novel's conclusion. For much of the novel, Frederic Henry oscillates between the feelings and thoughts of his two Italian friends, between the cynicism of Rinaldi and the hapless faith of a priest, between the satiric "snake of reason" (p. 170), and the frozen ritual of the priest's native region of Abruzzi, "where the roads were frozen and hard as iron, where it was clear cold and dry and the snow was dry and powdery and hare-tracks in the snow and the peasants took off their hats and called you Lord and there was good hunting" (p. 13). Setting Frederic Henry apart from his friends is his growing attraction to his fragile English heroine, where other moral dilemmas play out. Of special importance to Hemingway's artistic purpose, the love of an American for an English girl is finally issue-less. With Catherine's death, one finds the end to any attachment to European ideals. The romance and fascination for an overly refined and fragile culture has ended. As Hemingway wrote to Perkins when he began work on *A Farewell to Arms*: "I should have gone to America two years ago when I planned. I was through with Europe and needed to go to America before I could write the book that happened there" (*L*, p. 274). Through the formal experiments of his first two novels, Hemingway contested classical European values, both in a literary and a social sense, and cleared his way for the creation of new innovations.

Hemingway's interest and alliances dramatically shift in the work that follows *A Farewell to Arms*, as does, once again and in a visible fashion, the formal nature of his work. In this sense, *Death in the Afternoon* and *Green Hills of Africa* attest to the eclipse of European civilization and develop a view of tradition, and, implicitly, historical understanding that are radically at odds with traditional Western perceptions. In both works, the English are badly treated (with the exception of "Pop," a transplanted, Africanized Englishman), as Hemingway seeks what one might call a "native" tradition and a revitalized practice responsive to the demands of new country. Hemingway came to realize in the 1920s that the "part, if truly made, could represent the whole" (*DIA*, p. 278), and his specific native parts could stand in the place of a European artistic and intellectual exhaustion. Not only did the success of *A Farewell to Arms* give Hemingway the confidence to consciously reinscribe himself in an American context, but it allowed him, for a period of time, to resist the insistent demands of his contemporaries that he again take up external causes in defense of alienating values. The Key West period now begins.

Here, we might see that "decadence," like any "bogy," is a mere superstition, a fog seeming to harbor an impending doom. Hemingway urges his reader to penetrate the fog, to experience release as the fog lifts—as it always does—to enjoy the now sunny day and new opportunities that abound for mastery and willful action. Shortly, one attends a bullfight—likely the first—where one finds that mastery is present in periods of "decadence," that practices exist that value life, and that a bull, and the "bogy" of death, can be met on their own ground in a socially valid art form. And now that "decadence" has been encountered it is possible *to think*. Now, thought hinges on an actual event and does not circumscribe or distance life in advance. Still, some will not like it, but this eventuality does not deny the validity of that action covered and covered up by the term "decadence." Rather, what is unhinged is the axiological status of preconceptions.

*Part Two*

# "Its Fullest Flower at Its Rottenest Point"

*Chapter III*

# What You Make of It

*The bastards don't want you to joke because it disturbs their categories.*

Hemingway, *Letters*

*And then the transitions, the* sequence—*what an entanglement.*

Flaubert, *Letters*

Carlos Baker argues, defensively, that there are two possible uses of Hemingway's *tauromaquia*, as "quite likely the best (guide-book) of its kind in any language" and as a "sourcebook" useful in reading *For Whom the Bell Tolls*, which Baker considers Hemingway's masterpiece.[1] Yet, he has little to say about the "*tauromaquia*" *as a book*. Arthur Waldhorn suggests that the book exhibits "frontier values," a point he fails to develop, and concludes: "It is, at last, the work of a chastened, depressed writer."[2] Lastly, Earl Rovit, who developed any number of sensitive readings of Hemingway's works, makes use of *Death in the Afternoon* as a reference for Hemingway's aesthetics, a mother lode of useful citations.[3] The reason for this inattention on the part of good critics is twofold. Their more or less traditionalist perspective obscures the value of all that fails to conform to preestablished aesthetic criteria, especially with regard to acceptable genres. In Baker's words: *Death in the Afternoon* "is honest and realistic. It is even, in certain respects, straightforwardly reportorial, a fact which tells somewhat against it when compared with works of fictional art."[4] The other reason for undervaluing *Death in the Afternoon* is found in Rovit's assumption that Hemingway's "volumes of the 1930s were generally inferior production."[5] Among the best of Hemingway's readers, attitudes that unconsciously reflect Hemingway's bad reviews in the 1930s can still be found. Interestingly, an earlier political dissatisfaction with Hemingway's eccentric course in the 1930s arises anew, only now as aesthetic fault.

However, it remains possible to imagine *Death in the Afternoon* as inaugurating a second phase of Hemingway's career, one that, like the first, exhibited a range of heterogeneous works: a guide book, perhaps, but also a twined apprenticeship in every sense as decisive as the Paris years—different problems, different setting, and necessarily different adjustments. From a reader's point of view, *Death in the Afternoon* describes a practice found in a period alleged to be decadent, and, for this reason, unrepresentative and likely unrepresentable in being both immoral and exceptional. In this context, Hemingway's *tauromaquia* is preoccupied with our exposure to the "*inaccrochable*" of "Up in Michigan" and the violence of *In Our Time*, both preconditions to a "separate peace." As Hemingway explains at the beginning of *Death in the Afternoon*, his growing interest in the bullfight parallels his apprenticeship as a writer. Its agenda, disclosed after the success of *A Farewell to Arms*, is to educate his audience in an open work aligned with Bill Gorton's refreshing attitude discussed earlier. It manifests a positive response to the nihilistic consequences of WWI, because, by a stroke of luck—"fortuitous and inevitable"—Hemingway found in Spain the integral action that seemed denied in his experience of the war. And it is found in the "scandalous" bullfight, an institutionalized practice that has its own historical evolution.

Again, "a scarecrow, a bogy, a red herring"—such epithets best describe, according to Richard Gilman, the reactionary use of the word "decadence."[6] In *Death in the Afternoon*, Hemingway writes: "decadence is a difficult word to use because it has become little more than a term of abuse applied by critics to anything they do not yet understand or which seems to differ from their moral concepts" (pp. 70–71). These cautionary notes suggest the altered relationship of critical understanding and artistic production in periods of cultural transition. Accordingly, the critic is often badly situated to appreciate a transitional art because he or she thinks that the purpose of an action is to be understood and to represent preexisting cultural values. More often than not, in Hemingway's experience, critics sit in judgment, ready to legislate the artist's work based on something other than the work. Whatever value the word might have, decadence needs to be understood in terms of a full, integral action. When Hemingway raises the subject of decadence in *Death in the Afternoon*, he presents it in the context of the competition between Belmonte and Joselito, where "bullfighting for seven years had a golden age in spite of the fact that it was in the process of being destroyed" (p. 69). Numerous factors are at play during this period, but the most surprising among them is Hemingway's insistence on the primary cause: "It is the decadence of the modern bull that has made modern bullfighting possible." At an earlier time, bullfighters faced more mature bulls, "which were brought to the highest point of physical force, strength, knowledge . . . and general difficulty and danger." In the modern period, bulls are "bred down in size . . . the length of their horns" shortened. Because of this modification, Belmonte and Joselito can work closer to the bull. The emphasis shifts from the killing of the bull, the older "moment of truth," "to the technique developed by Belmonte." As Hemingway observes, "as the *corrida* has developed and decayed there has been less emphasis on the form of killing, which was once the whole thing, and more on cape work, the placing of the *banderillas* and the work with the *muleta*. The cape, the *banderillas* and the *muleta* have all become ends in themselves rather than a means to an end and the bullfight has both lost and gained thereby" (p. 67). Belmonte's "genius," given the "material" at hand, lies in his ability to break the rules: he "could *torear*." Then, with the arrival of Joselito and his competition with Belmonte, one finds a further transformation: "Anyway, the decadent, the impossible, the almost depraved, style of Belmonte was grafted and grown into the great healthy, intuitive genius of Joselito."

This summary of Hemingway's discussion serves a dual purpose. It allows us, through "transplanting," to better understand the nature of Hemingway's immediate artistic situation and the "matter" at hand against which he, too, broke the rules of his predecessors. For a variety of reasons, the modern novel, as seen earlier, has been "bred down," and it is the reduced version of the work, as a "minor" literature, that allows a radical artistic shift from the traditional "moment of truth" to cape work, etc. (about which more is said below, in the discussion of "A Natural History of the Dead"). Implicitly, Hemingway acknowledges his certain identity as a decadent writer, along with his contemporaries, who face "bred down bulls." Yet, there remains a choice: the impossible, the almost depraved style of Belmonte "or the great healthy, intuitive genius of Joselito."

The present, as found in the bullfight and in Hemingway's literary circumstances, is of central importance, but his preoccupation, his investigation, also involves the historical conditions that continue to inform the present.[7] This focus of understanding has a definite intention: the possibility of meaningful action in the present and, with respect to artistic practice, a narrowed but particular freedom. Hemingway does not deny the fact that he exists and works in a decadent period, but he questions, i.e., "problematizes," the assumptions that underlie this concept, concerning, in particular, an attitude of passivity in a context of cultural degeneration. His analysis of bullfighting as an action and as institution speaks to that recognition and the validation of his own artistic direction. Mastery and skill, in a visible theatre, and a shift of focus are still possible, even given decadent conditions. The present, as seen by Hemingway, is an unstable mixture of forces, a conflicted space of gains and losses.

After the publication of *Death in the Afternoon*, Hemingway wrote to Everett Perry, a city librarian in Los Angeles, to answer his objections to the book's use of "plain words":

> I am trying, always, to convey to the reader a full and complete feeling of the thing I am dealing with; to make the person reading feel it has happened to them. In doing this I have to use many expedients, which, if they fail, seem needlessly shocking. Because it is very hard to do I must sometimes fail. But I might fail with one reader and succeed with another. (*L*, pp. 380–81)

The intensification of experience, a "complete feeling of the thing," involves and works against the effects of decadence. "Many expedients" are required, since traditional, time-tested rules and practices are invalidated precisely because they are a product of decadence, as conditions responsible for the present impasse. Correspondingly, the writer shifts his public role as spokesman and safeguard of cultural values and can no longer be sheltered in the customary role of mastery and wisdom. Freed of his paternal role, he makes do with expedients, allows himself to stumble and recover. This, too, is an aspect of the author's newfound simplicity, to speak in a direct and precise fashion only about things he knows, and knows because they arise from his experience, and through intensified emotional experience, establishes a new relationship to his readers. Neither patronizing nor overly concerned with popularity in *Death in the Afternoon*, Hemingway saw this work as an open site. Assuredly, Hemingway continued to contest the dominant values of his culture, but he also revived the struggle that gives value to human affairs.

The question of decadence is as much political as aesthetic. Consider the debate between Brecht and Georg Lukács in the 1930s. Aware of the prospect of failure and against Lukács's charge of decadence, Brecht insisted on the need for experimentation: "I am speaking from experience when I say that one need not be afraid to produce daring, unusual things for the proletariat so long as they deal with real situations."[8] Brecht pointed out the "bogy" at the heart of Lukács's critique: "Production makes them uncomfortable. You never know where you are with production; production is the unforeseeable. You never know what's going to come out."[9] Of consequence, Brecht's ideal audience is not inhibited by "unforeseeable" prospects:

> They found some things superfluous which the artists declared to be necessary; but then they were generous and not against excess; on the contrary they were against those who were superfluous. They did not put a muzzle on a willing horse but they saw that it pulled its weight. They did not believe in such things as "the" method. They knew that many methods were necessary to attain their goals.[10]

The next chapter will return to the critical reception of *Death in the Afternoon* and the effect this had on the works that followed his *tauromaquia*. It is useful to recall, however, that Hemingway's "production" did not find a willing audience and the first reviews were indeed critical. This negative reception concerned a book that he had planned as early as 1925, a "sort of Doughty's *Arabia Deserta,*" instead of the "used up" novel form (*L*, p. 156). *Death in the Afternoon* was meant to be different, to break with "the" method, to be daring, to be excessive. It is perhaps in the nature of digressions to effect the reversal Hemingway intended. Roland Barthes addresses the two related ways of dislodging the power that hides in language:

> Since, as I have tried to suggest, this teaching has as its object discourse taken in the inevitability of power, method can really bear only on the means of loosening, baffling, or at the very least, of lightening this power. And I am increasingly convinced, both in writing and in teaching, that the fundamental operation of this loosening method is, if one writes, fragmentations, and if one teaches, digression, or, to put it in a preciously ambiguous word, *excursion.*[11]

Digression is among Hemingway's "expediencies," no different in intention than the anecdote discussed earlier. It disrupts the monologue of authority, reveals the vagaries of the moment, the contingency of situations. Seemingly ephemeral, digression engages the real as it flashes. Like an anecdote, it welcomes its eventual disappearance, in its exposure to the moment and exposure of the speaker. A supreme risk and a source of pleasure, digression fulfills the meaning of Brecht's aphorism: "A deep need makes for a superficial grasp."[12]

## 2

Hemingway said that *Death in the Afternoon* embodies his "literary credo" (*L*, p. 362). More than being *about* his literary beliefs, it embodies those beliefs *as* writing and *in* its specific formal structure. Maxwell Perkins thought the book wonderful, as he confided to Fitzgerald: "Ernest's book is a very fine book. In some ways it is his best and biggest book. It is very revealing too because it gives a whole point of view about life in giving one about bull fighting, directly, and much more by inference. And there are beautiful things in it about America, as well as Spain."[13] Perkins had felt that *Death in the Afternoon* succeeded because it was "architecture, not interior decoration" (p. 191), simultaneously, the expression and embodiment of a singular practice. More directly, the book involves the fusion of knowledge and practice in an indisputably finite setting. In his "introduction," Hemingway draws an analogy between the appreciation of wine and bullfighting:

> Wine is one of the most civilized things in the world and one of the natural things of the world that has been brought to the greatest perfection, and it offers a greater range for enjoyment and appreciation than, possibly, any other purely sensory thing which may be purchased.
>
> One can learn about wines and pursue the education of one's palate with great enjoyment all of a lifetime, the palate becoming more educated and capable of appreciation and you having constantly increasingly enjoyment and appreciation of wine even though the kidneys may weaken, the big toe become painful, the finger joints stiffen, until finally, just when you love it the most you are finally forbidden wine entirely. (p. 10)

Being sensory, Hemingway's education is individualistic and involves individual appreciation, but it is also limited by the fact that the individual possesses a kidney and a big toe. The opportunities for knowledge and pleasure and their ultimate limitations are inextricably mixed for the "naturalist," Hemingway's own self-definition; and, if nature makes available sensory experience, it correspondingly exacts a price. Yet, wine is also a civilized product, and it shows how nature can be "brought to the greatest perfection," not through substituting the "picturesque" but by distilling the "nature" in nature, as found in the plain-bottled, full-bodied Grand crus of Medoc. Clarity and full-bodied expression, then, are the objectives of Hemingway's education, whether in wine appreciation, in bullfighting, or in writing. An education of a lifetime, it begins in nature, seeks perfection from nature, leaves behind, with luck, plain-bottled vintages that can be of use to later generations in their sensory education to the pleasures of life. From an individual standpoint, another "moment of truth" occurs when, fully involved in life and caught up in the movement of bringing out life's greatest perfection, nature reasserts itself.

*Death in the Afternoon*, through its digressive method and because of its digressions, records an obsession. Of course, it is about bullfighting and it shows how Hemingway came to love bullfighting, but, far more, it is his book of life, of the obsession life becomes, especially because "life is something that comes before death" (p. 266). Writing an impossible *Pilgrim's Progress*, Hemingway leads the reader to "the moment of truth," a peak of emotional intensity that is both the highest pitch of emotional intensity and a profound absence, since "the moment of truth" is no longer tied to a sacred dimension that lies beyond it—only finitude.

It is assumed the reader begins in ignorance, or with certain pre-conceptions, about bullfights, about life, and about a different artistic creation. Thus, the reader is asked (at the beginning of chapter 7) to witness and to experience the spectacle in actuality. Many refuse the invitation, while others return from the experience disgusted. The few who remain now, who have passed a threshold experience, begin their education. Knowledge increases in proportion to the openness of feeling brought to one's life, until knowledge and feeling are merged in a final stage of total obsession: "and just when you love it the most you are finally forbidden [it] entirely." The end of this experience contains no "wow," transcendental truth, or revelation as reward for the initiated. More precisely, the end result for the few is an intensifica-tion of life, but within an encompassing absence. As a modern "event," the bullfight is fully secularized. Still, it maintains the ves-tiges of an older perspective, an archaic dimension where "the moment of truth" was continuous with a mystic elevation, where the ritual sacrifice of the bull was linked to the ineffable. As a secularized action, the modern bullfight recaptures this moment, but in a move-ment that returns us to finite existence. The body is given the last word in the modern scene, but it also achieves its own elevation and satisfaction. Such considerations account for the dynamic of modern bullfighting, which obscure the traditional importance given to the final act. Classical conditions no longer hold, the traditional end of the spectacle is subverted, and "the moment of truth" is found in the severe confines of finite existence.

Once the individual has experienced a first shock and once it is known that life is individual and terminal, it is more than possible to adapt to these irrevocable conditions with courage and humor. With the "*novillada*" stage behind us, immediately the comic intrudes in the figure of the Old Lady, who "liked to see the bulls hit the horses" because it seemed "homey" (p. 64). She is called a "mystic" by the author and made a part of the book. Thus, Hemingway begins his

travesty of the Old Lady's somewhat dignified pose and, more generally, the decorum of a classical book. At first, the comic perception of
*Death in the Afternoon* is allied with an encompassing cynicism, a
complementary response to a first goring. The reader (thanks to the
Old Lady) is invited to enter the real world of the Café Fornos, "fre-
quented only by people connected with the bullfight and by whores.
There is smoke, hurrying of waiters, noise of glasses and you have the
noisy privacy of a big café" (p. 64). The Café Fornos is another of
Hemingway's "clean, well-lighted places":

> There are bullfighters at every table and for all tastes and all the
> people in the café live off bullfighters in some way or another. A
> shark rarely has more than four remoras or sucking fish that fasten
> to him or swim to him or swim with him, but a bullfighter, when he
> is making money, has dozens. (pp. 64–65)

Exploitation is the norm and Hemingway has numerous examples of
bullfighters who allow external factors to influence their performance
in the ring. The mark of the genuine bullfighter, however, is his
capacity to distance himself from the "sucking fish" and much else:
"the measure of his detachment of course is the measure of his imagination and always on the day of the fight and finally during the whole
end of the season, there is a detached something in their minds that
you can almost see" (p. 56). As a professional activity, the bullfight
operates in the two distinct, yet interrelated worlds, of commerce and
art, as does the writing profession. Needless to say, the health of the
spectacle and the vitality of writing depend on the integrity of their
principle agents.

With the introduction of the "Old Lady," Hemingway structures
his exposition in two connected ways, i.e., with respect to the individual chapters and their sequence. Responding to the Old Lady's
desires (and carrying throughout her presence in the book), the typical chapter begins with a practical discussion followed by an attempt
on the "author's" part to relieve the Old Lady's boredom or to enter-
tain her, providing "her money's worth," with stories, anecdotes,
seemingly irrelevant comments, and the like. These end pieces are
largely unrelated to bullfighting. The chapter format, then, is practical
exposition followed by an entertaining application of the prior lesson

in a different context—act and reenactment. Overall the reenactment, it seems fair to say, usually fails with the Old Lady, as it fails, as well, to recapture and adequately re-present the opening business of a particular chapter. (This technique will be considered more fully in the discussion of *Green Hills of Africa*.) The second improvisation involves the sequence of the chapters and it, too, is conditioned by the presence of the Old Lady. Simple and direct, we are given a description and analysis of different bullfighters (chapters 7–10), followed by four chapters (chapters 11–14) that describe aspects of the bull's nurture, conditioning, and so forth, and finally, the first two parts are brought together in the bullfight itself (chapters 15–19). Schematically, the three parts of the book that follow the introduction explore: 1) the nature of the bullfighter's knowledge, skill, and courage; 2) the pure force and aleatory *nature* of the bull; and 3) the instruments of the bullfight and their technical use that ground, in mechanical sequence, the separate "acts" of the bullfight. Both devices of Hemingway's organization are purely heuristic, and it may be a part of Hemingway's purpose to show the artificiality of any representative scheme that tries to express what can only be experienced. Yet, without instruction, a person going to a bullfight for the first time who is lucky to see "the ideal bull and the ideal fighter for that bull . . . would be so confused, visually, by the many things he was seeing that he could not take it all in with his eyes, and something which he might never see again in his life would mean no more to him than a regular performance" (p. 14).

Since it is meant to provide an education, *Death in the Afternoon* begins with the familiar, with a presentation of individual bullfighters, a gradual leading of the Old Lady to an appreciation of the unfamiliar complexity of a seemingly barbarous pastime. The Old Lady finds aspects of the bullfight "homey" and she likes to observe bullfighters and to talk about them. Of consequence to Hemingway's purpose, this attraction results from decadence: "Individuals are interesting, Madame, but they are not all. In this case it is because, with the decadence of bullfighting, it has become altogether a matter of the individual" (p. 85). In one way or another, this discussion suggests the modern reality of artistic creation, a new and more decisive concern for Hemingway.

Concerning the Old Lady's preferences and, by extension, that of a literary audience that enjoys the prominence given to the novelist, a principle of domestication is at work and this "instinctual" identification is also the product of a modern degeneration. As the bullfight becomes better understood, it establishes its difference from the Old Lady's desires and can no longer be contained by her normative and reductive perceptions. In time, the Old Lady rejects the "strangeness" of the spectacle and significantly alters her original, deferential stance toward the author. Her resistance to the bullfight matches her blindness toward the "otherness" of her own culture, as witness in the unexpected outbreak of senseless violence in WWI depicted in "A Natural History of the Dead." In comparing the bullfight, and, by extension, the Spanish ethos to Western practices, the author's and the Old Lady's culture seems the worse, more violent and self-destructive. Thus, the end chapters center on the author's cultural background now deprived of its idealistic pretensions and focuses on personal and artistic pathologies. For example, Hemingway's negative portraits of T. S. Eliot and Aldous Huxley focus on disembodied intellectuality, the obverse of the Spanish emphasis on an essentially violent and haphazard nature and a developed artistic medium based on this recognition. Hemingway's end of chapter discussions are not gratuitous, as so many of Hemingway's early critics have said. Rather, they are intrinsic to his sense of a valid modern artistic activity. As importantly, they present a condition for achieving human dignity in artistic activity that acknowledges finite nature.

"What might they think of me?"—this question had to have occurred to Hemingway. He knew what was expected and was aware that he was writing against the grain. "What we want in a book by this citizen is people talking," he writes, "that is all he knows how to do and now he doesn't do it. The fellow is no philosopher, no savant, an incompetent zoologist, he drinks too much and cannot punctuate readily and now he had stopped writing dialogue. Some one ought to put a stop to him. He is bull crazy" (p. 120). The novelist goes wildly astray in pretending his activity is a serious one. But it might be as much the case that from the point of view of a real bull in an actual bull ring and the kind of writing Hemingway was struggling to achieve, philosophy, scholarship, and science are, themselves, out of touch. Spain, with respect to Western attitudes of the time, appears as a world of play, however violent; and, oppositely, philosophy dissolves in a world of play.[14] Indeed, Hemingway is "bull crazy." To favor Spain is to choose transgression over respectability. However, the risk goes far deeper, since Hemingway's purpose in exposing himself to ridicule is to experience, in Georges Batailles' words, "the summit of being." Bataille writes: "the summit of being only fully reveals itself, *in its wholeness*, in a transgressive movement where the form of thinking that is based on work and the expansion of consciousness ultimately surpasses work, knowing it can no longer subjugate itself."[15]

> I went to Spain to see the bullfights and to try to write about them for myself. I thought they would be simple and barbarous and cruel and that I would not like them, but that I would see certain action which would give me the feeling of life and death that I was working for. I found the definite action; but the bullfight was so far from simple and I liked it so much that it was much too complicated for my then equipment for writing to deal with . . . (p. 3)

Moreover, Hemingway's desire was triggered by snapshots shown to him by Gertrude Stein of Joselito "in the ring and herself and Alice Toklas in the first row of wooden *barreras* at the bull ring in Valencia . . ." (p. 1). Miss Stein's picture seems emblematic of the writer's initial stance of superiority to the bullfighter. As a minor pastime, bullfighting is easily subsumed in the writer's more serious purpose. However, it soon reveals itself as a limiting case of the writer's *work*, as an ideal that is impossible to achieve, as seen in Bill Gorton's remark in *The Sun Also Rises*: "Tell him, I'm ashamed of being a writer" (p. 175). What becomes of a writer who is made aware that books are often written out of egotism? What of the authority of the writer's stance? What practice can he adopt? Certain answers are readily available at this point. Like the bullfighter, a writer must have full command of his "equipment" and "that detached something in (his) mind that you can almost see"; he must risk himself for his writing within the existing rules and break those rules if necessary; he must avoid demagogy and mystification and attempt, always, to produce a clear statement without tricks. Finally, he will know that "a serious writer is not to be confounded with a solemn writer" (p. 192). If the author is Hemingway, he produces "A Natural History of the

Dead," a centerpiece of *Death in the Afternoon*, the telling of which compels the Old Lady to say, "You know I like you less and less the more I know you" (p. 144). The story bears close attention.

"A Natural History of the Dead" is brief and made up entirely of dialogue, a fact not without meaning, given Hemingway's earlier self-characterization, but it is introduced within an elaborate frame that delays, even obstructs, its ever beginning. The story is announced after a long discussion of fighting bulls, their bravery and violence in the natural state. Once its title is given, the story is positioned as an example of the genre of natural history, with Mungo Park cited as a principal practitioner. This allows an apparently whimsical author to start to record his observations of WWI. The Old Lady is not amused. "Be patient, can't you?" the author responds. "It's very hard to write like this" (p. 135). In effect, the introductory frame shows that natural histories, as written by W. H. Hudson, Bishop Stanley, and Mungo Park, had been "historical" only in the sense that they reflected the presuppositions of the late nineteenth century. As works of natural observation, they added something beyond actual observations. Lost in the desert, a seemingly natural desolation, Mungo Park discovers a flower that immediately restores his assurance in his historical destiny:

> Can that being who planted, watered and brought to perfection, in this obscure part of the world, a thing which appears of so little importance, look with unconcern upon the situation of creatures formed after his image? (p. 136)

Elsewhere in *Death in the Afternoon*, Hemingway had denounced the "one-visit book" written about the bullfight because of its "erectile writing" and "bedside mysticism." He explains his reservations: "all objects (in that portentous state) look different. They are slightly larger, more mysterious, and vaguely blurred" (p. 53). Mungo Park, too, adds to the thing observed, interprets it to supplement a lack. If Hemingway, on the contrary, observes poverty, he seeks a plain statement and the law that accounts for it; he does not add "a little subjectivity." In his own observation, the author of "A Natural History of the Dead" (which naturally includes the prior histories of the now dead W. H. Hudson, Bishop Stanley, and Mungo Park) finds no self-

evident network of rationality, no image of creation or the Creator—
only unclassifiable exceptions, "it being amazing that the human body
should be blown into pieces which exploded along no anatomical
lines, but rather, divided as capriciously as fragmentation in the burst
of a high explosive shell." The dead bodies on a battlefield or those of
women at an exploded munitions factory are shocking, but as
unnerving in that "burst" is a revelation of *nothing*, no implicit
meaning outside decomposing fragments of dead bodies, no plan,
divine or otherwise, but an excessive, maddening reality irreducible to
a single meaning.

Mungo Park finds hope in the desert because he brings to his
experience external values. Much the same can be said of Whittier's
*Snow Bound*, which is presented as an influence of the author's story.
(It is another of Hemingway's partial misdirections, when he says that
his story is "written in popular style and is designed to be the Whittier's *Snow Bound* of our time . . ." p. 133.) The natural history of
Mungo Park, and, equally, Whittier's apocrypha circulate in polite
society because they maintain extra-literary values, taste, proportion,
decorum, truth, and naturalness. Hemingway, however, has no sub-
text and he negates these constraints and their surreptitious connection to a "natural" home. On the success of his writing rests another
definition of "literature," a multiplication of exceptions, indecorous
and ludic.[16] Leading up to his story, Hemingway refers to Goya twice
as an exemplary model and he likely intends the following question:
What is literature in "The Sleep of Reason"? Later in the book, Hemingway points to another aspect of Goya's production: "Goya was
like Stendhal; the sight of a priest could stimulate either of those good
anti-clericals into a rage of production. Goya's crucifixion is a cyni-
cally romantic, wooden oleograph that could serve as a poster for the
announcement of crucifixions in the manner of bullfight posters" (p.
204). The first part of "A Natural History of the Dead" enacts Goya's
cynicism in its handling of Mungo Park and traditional natural histories, while the story, itself, works out the darker perceptions that conditioned Goya's ridicule of "clerical" attitudes.

Like Goya's *Caprichos*, the story involves a violent exchange
between a doctor and a young field officer. It begins with the bare fact,
the incongruous fact, of a soldier who is dying and who has been
placed in a cave reserved for the dead. The doctor can do nothing; the

dying man's "head was broken as a flowerpot may be broken, although it was all held together by membranes and a skillfully applied bandage now soaked and hardened, with the structure of his brain disturbed by a piece of broken steel in it" (p. 141). Lying among the dead, he disturbs the stretcher-bearers, who urge the doctor to return to the cave: "he looked at him twice: once in the daylight, once with a flashlight. That would have made a good etching for Goya, the visit with the flashlight, I mean." Thus illuminated, the scene is imponderable. "What do you want me to do about it?" asks the doctor. Part of its disturbance is caused by the absence of a framework that could give it meaning. It is little more than a curious lighting of the dark, something black, unclassifiable. Only the ensuing demand of the artillery officer, "Why don't you give him an overdose of morphine?" keeps it from fading into oblivion. This interjection has little to do with the fate of the dying man, since he dies at the moment the question is asked. Nevertheless, a question, never answerable, now leads to other equally difficult questions that concern values, personal responsibility, and authority:

> "Who are you to ask me questions? Are you my superior? Are you in command of this dressing post? Do me the courtesy to answer."

Command, not courtesy, is at stake in this confrontation. At any rate, any pretense to civility is shattered by the next outburst:

> "F_ _k yourself," said the artillery officer.
> "So," said the doctor. "So, you said that. All right. All right. We shall see."
> The lieutenant of artillery stood up and walked toward him.
> "F_ _k yourself," he said. "F_ _k yourself. F_ _k your mother. F_ _k your sister . . ."

The doctor reacts by throwing iodine in the officer's eyes:

> "I'll kill you," he said. "I'll kill you as soon as I can see."
> "I am the boss," said the doctor. "All is forgiven since you know I am the boss . . ."

The doctor is finally told that the dying man has died:

> "See, my poor lieutenant? We dispute about nothing. In time of war we dispute about nothing."
>
> "Nothing," says the doctor, as he recaptures the fellow feeling and saving grace of "my poor lieutenant."

In the chapter that contains "A Natural History of the Dead," Hemingway describes the spontaneous violence of bulls when fighting for mastery: "I have seen them fight again and again for small causes that I was not able to make out." The fight usually ends with the mutual recognition of the superiority of one or the other; "Once though, in the corrals after a fight in which one bull turned away admitting he was beaten, the other followed him and charged, getting the horn in the defeated bull's flank and throwing him over. . . . The defeated bull got to his feet once, wheeled to face head-on, but in the first horn exchange he was caught in the eye, then went down under another charge" (p. 127). The violence at the dressing post duplicates the bull's natural struggle for dominance, except that the human action superimposes a second reality onto the first, one which may seem more basic to human nature, but which seems little more than a nervous reaction to excessive behavior—"All is forgiven since you know I am the boss." Pity, as a saving gesture, results from the doctor's "victory," and it rises from the "depths" where the doctor finds a consolation that partly resolves a savage encounter. What, at this moment, are we to make of Mungo Park's assertion of "creatures formed after his image"?

"A Natural History of the Dead" shows how values that were once external to literature, as silent reference and as guaranteeing an implicit meaning, are now transformed into ironic by-products of literary production, and, for the doctor, a transparent ruse that allows him to regain his self-possession. Genuine authority for Hemingway arises from an autonomous action where the individual stands unassisted and it cannot be confused with the doctor's charitable offer, one that masks his guilt over a lapse of professional behavior. He meant well, of course, and he was provoked; and, he did vanquish his opponent. Sadly, none of this matters; and, besides, the doctor was unequipped, by profession and by his Hippocratic oath, for the kind of life found in a fully naturalized history. Having to place life before death, he is in no position to relish the force of Nietzsche's contention that "the living is merely a type of what is dead, and a very rare type."[17] He is at a particular loss in a war and in a setting of ubiquitous death. Overworked and fatigued, circumstanced by exceptions that are the rule, the doctor loses control, and his assertion of authority, understandable from a personal standpoint, divests authority of its sacrosanct character. What gives credence, now, to an action? In the doctor's example, we see authority stuck on to the tail of an action or obscuring the cowardly act that made him the "boss." Hemingway's lesson and practice differ radically from Mungo Park's. "A Natural History of the Dead" is a pure event with nothing added, a crafted dialogue without flowery coda. The event in the story or the story as event is left as it was found, a "natural" document.

One's first experience of the bullfight is a rite of passage to a far larger world. The appreciation of wine opens a world of taste and pleasure. And "A Natural History of the Dead" underlines the importance of sensations and feeling, the experience of feeling "more than you know." Hemingway's story shows characters caught in a transgressive action, going far beyond ordinary behavior, crossing the line of civility, yet the end result as story is an intensification of feelings that overrides common sense. With regard to this process of intensification, we find another rite of passage, only now as an opening to Hemingway's aesthetics. Again, his intention is to contest classical modes of representation from his marginalized perspective by giving us the brute language of a wartime encounter, with the end result of indigestible feelings.

As readers, we were asked at the beginning of chapter 7 to witness our first bullfight. We've seen the horses badly gored and a bull has been killed. A dangerous transition is required since we first encountered the bullfighting world of the Café Fornos. As an initial consequence, one observes stupidity at every turn, a leveling uniformity, and a belittling "it all comes down to the same thing." The Café Fornos or a dressing station at the front in WWI show the collapse of distinctions—between life and death, authority and cowardice, decorum and viciousness. Within either the realities of war or the Café Fornos, nihilism leads to the negation of individual will and the devaluation of action. There is room, of course, for amused observation, since curiosities abound:

> *Old Lady*: You mean?
> Not exactly, but something of the sort.
> *Old Lady*: You mean he - - - - - -?
> . . .
> *Old Lady*: It repelled me from the first.

The discussion of decadence at the end of chapter 7 involved Raymond Radiguet and his "literary protector," Jean Cocteau. The story is about Cocteau's anger at Radiguet when he began to show an interest in women, "*Bebe est vicieuse—il aime les femmes*" (p. 171). Another perversion caps the anecdote:

> . . . But what finally happened to the late Radiguet ?
> He caught typhoid from swimming in the Seine and
> died from it.
> *Old Lady*: Poor chap.
> Poor chap, indeed. (p. 72)

Set against this anecdote is a more positive perception of decadence, as found in the new circumstances of bullfighting.

We again note Hemingway's equivocation in defining the modern bullfight: "Bullfighting has developed, or decayed, with emphasis increasingly placed on the manner of execution of the various passes rather than their effect." Decay or development? The modern— perhaps, any period of change—involves a displacement, both development and decay. We've seen the contours of this transition earlier; now we can focus on the two factors that combine to produce this transition to the modern bullfight: "genius" and physical limitations. And the responsible agent is Belmonte, who "worked that way because of his lack of stature, his lack of strength, because of his feeble legs. He did not accept any rules without testing whether they might be broken, and he was a genius and a great artist. The way Belmonte worked was not a heritage, not a development; it was a revolution" (p. 69). Practicality and, of course, talent are embodied in Belmonte's genius, and, if he tested every rule, it is because his physical stature prevented him from performing in the traditional way. As importantly, though, in the emergence of modernism, Joselito enters the scene to compete with Belmonte: "Joselito learned it, and during the years of their competition, when they each had around a hundred *corridas* a year, he used to say, 'They say that he, Belmonte, works closer to the bull. It looks as though he does. But it isn't true. I really work closer. But it is more natural so it doesn't look so close.'" From their competition arises a modern "golden age," a complex state that reaches "its fullest flower at its rottenest point, which is the present" (p. 68). Typically, Hemingway observes, "there is no going back in the matter of sensations" (p. 69); and, after Belmonte and Joselito, formalism becomes all important, self-consciously everything, since it is through formal cape work and the experimentation with form that the artist exposes himself to the greatest danger and since it is the bull-fighter's ability with the cape or the *muleta* that establishes his professional ranking.

The cape had formerly served as a means of defense. Then, its function was extended to running the bull, protecting the men in the ring, and distracting the bull "when any bullfighter had gotten himself into a compromising position" (p. 174). The cape still remained a defensive instrument, but the elaboration of its use also increased the dangers it invited. What revolutionized cape work and began the modern bullfight was Belmonte's insight that cape work could be made consciously the moment of supreme danger. Physically weak and an indifferent killer, Belmonte reoriented his substantial limitations into a productive emphasis on the cape as an end in itself, and, thus, the modern bullfight arose, as a flowering of negative circumstances: "there has been no decadence in bullfighting in the use of the cape. There has not been a renaissance, but steady and complete improvement" (p. 176). Consequently, a redefinition of the "moment of truth,"

> where the horns almost touch, and sometimes do touch, his thighs while the bull's shoulder's touch his chest, with no move of defense against death that goes by in the horns except the slow movement of his arms and his judgment of distance; these passes are finer than any cape work of the past and as emotional as anything can be. (p. 175)

From a literary standpoint, an integral modern line exists, where the greatest risk and exposure is regrounded in stylistic innovation and experimentation (not the end, but from a traditional standpoint, the means of writing), and it begins in the revolution initiated by three masters of style: Ezra Pound, Gertrude Stein, and James Joyce. For writers of Hemingway's generation, they are the legacy from which "there was no going back," and for Hemingway, they establish the only possible beginning. Joyce is most readily identified with Belmonte, both because he tested every rule of writing and almost single-handedly revolutionized literature and because of his physical limitations, bad eyesight, and his compensating "genius." Who might Joselito be in the context of modern writing? Is it Hemingway who saw himself as competing with Joyce and "who worked closer to the bull"? Perhaps, thinking of himself, "it doesn't look so close" because his style was more "natural." Clearly, Joselito is the modern ideal of the artist, but we very likely find Hemingway in the admiring description of Maera and a more modest self-portrait: "his presence in the ring raised the whole thing from the least effort, get-rich-quick, wait-for-the-mechanical bull basis it had fallen to, and, while he was in the ring, it again had dignity and passion. . . . He gave emotion always, and finally, as he steadily improved his style, he was an artist" (pp. 78–79).

As an analysis of "means," *Death in the Afternoon* is an honest book. It aims to educate the reader so that he can appreciate what is involved in the steady improvement of style. It teaches the reader what to look at and how to look, it being understood that the simplest observation requires discrimination. Hemingway's descriptions are from the ground up, there to be seen, since the vitality of an institution adheres to its details. A writer, at any rate, "will not be better than his audience very long. If they prefer tricks to sincerity they soon get the tricks. If a really good (writer) is to come and to remain honest, sincere, without tricks and mystifications there must be a nucleus of spectators he can play to when he comes" (p. 163). *Death in the Afternoon* is not about another interpretation of modernism. Rather its intent is to define a form of "rarity," situated in a specific time. The surface phenomena of the bullfight concerns Hemingway, not a possible rationalization found in the "mystical" depths of interpretation. Hemingway's position on the bullfight can be productively compared to Foucault's definition of discourse as a counterweight to interpretation: "it appears as an asset—finite, limited, desirable, useful—that has its own rules of appearance, but also its own conditions of appropriation and operation; an asset that consequently, from the moment of its existence (and not only in its 'practical application') poses the question of power; an asset that is, by nature, the object of struggle, a political struggle."[18]

Hemingway was criticized for ignoring the political struggles of the 1930s, but it may be that he saw politics extending through all the activities that give substance to a society, that he understood power, in other words, as polymorphous and ubiquitous. Consequently, *Death in the Afternoon* may be Hemingway's first guerrilla action for the Spanish cause against those who occlude their situation by charging their opponents with decadence. To recognize the contestation contained in the word "decadence" is to emphasize the desirability of the contested object. In the victory of either side lie the fate of literature and the viability of the modern as the space of struggle.

Historical sense is needed to overcome the nostalgia of those who monumentalize the past, who wish to see the modern as still-born:

> And it seems as though things were very different in those days and the bullfighters must have been such men as were the football players on the high-school team when we were still in grammar school. Things change very much and instead of great athletes only children play on the high-school teams now and if you sit with the older men at the café you know there are no good bullfighters now either; they are all children without honor, skill, or virtue, much the same as those children who now play football, a feeble game it has become, on the high-school team and nothing like the great, mature, sophisticated athletes in canvas-elbowed jerseys, smelling vinegary from sweated shoulder pads, carrying leather headguards, their moleskins clotted with mud, that walked on the leather-cleated shoes that printed in the earth along beside the sidewalk in the dusk, a long time ago. (p. 183)

The age of heroes, of demi-gods, of heroics is gone; and the past was always, irrevocably, the age of heroes. As for the present, it seems a diminished sport played by children. The past continues to haunt the present and inhibit present actions. When Hemingway said, "all bad writers are in love with the epic" (p. 54), he was thinking of the debilitating force of nostalgia and also the impossibility, for the present, of returning to a seemingly better time, an origin which is always the goal of epic circularity. But the passage above is not a simple opposition of past and present or a straightforward rejection of nostalgia. Rather, it begins with a disputable opposition and transforms it into the pathos of an ephemeral event, more feeling and intensification. After the beautifully descriptive "canvas-elbowed jerseys, smelling vinegary from sweated shoulder pads . . . the leather-cleated shoes that printed in the earth along beside the sidewalk in the dusk," we begin to believe in a world of "a long time ago." What could never have been now exists; and, it exists now as then, because of the particularity of physical detail, because of the smell and the sweat and the clotted mud, that stand for engagement in a present that had been the past. Hemingway's portrait of Joselito, a modern hero and "demi-god," has the same attention to detail and specific struggles, as does his initial definition of writing as exertion, the basis, as well, of his reservation regarding Gertrude Stein and Ezra Pound when their discipline slackened. Heroic actions are recoverable in the present, always within a limited sphere requiring sweat and struggle. It is not a question of the finite individual burdened by a monumental past, but the necessity to seize the past as a limited asset, as the prints left by leather-cleated shoes "beside the sidewalk in the dusk, a long time ago." Thus, for Hemingway:

> Every novel which is truly written contributes to the total knowledge which is there at the disposal of the next writer who comes, but the next writer must pay, always, a certain nominal percentage in experience to be able to understand and assimilate what is available as his birth-right and what he must, in turn, take his departure from. (p. 192)

3

We are close to the end, but, of course, there is no end, certainly nothing we could comfortably call a "wow." The last sentences of *Death in the Afternoon* tell us: "No. It is not enough of a book, but still there were a few things to be said. There were a few practical things to be said" (p. 278). After "A Natural History of the Dead," we find the following exchange:

> *Old Lady*: Is that the end? I thought you said it was like John Greenleaf Whittier's *Snow Bound*.
>     Madame, I'm wrong again. We aim so high and yet we miss the target. (p. 144)

What was it we witnessed in the last rays of sunshine of a Spanish afternoon, in the dusk after a football game, after the violence at a dressing post in WWI, or, finally, throughout the epilogue of *Death in the Afternoon*? Was it the last day of judgment or the first day of creation? The throes of a savage birth or the gasps of an expiring culture?

*Death in the Afternoon* was a transitional book for Hemingway; indeed, a book of transitions, the fragmented parts of the present pathos of life as lived. It is an education and a testimony to the fact that the present contains the power to produce memorable images (which, in turn, are dealt with by future generations). What began as a diversion for Hemingway came in time to reinforce his "necessity" as a writer. "I know things change now," writes Hemingway, "and I do not care. It's all been changed for me. Let it all change" (p. 278). The epilogue to *Death in the Afternoon* is charged with the perception of changing time: the once delightful view of the mountains outside Pamplona is now obstructed by new apartment buildings; Navarra had been "all the color of wheat" and "now clouds come fast in shadows over wheat"; the Guardia Civil, who had been friendly and helped him when he lost his train tickets, have changed in the new political climate; *La Libertad* is now like *Le Temps*. Storytelling also has known simpler times:

> In front of the barn a woman held a duck whose throat she had cut and stroked him gently while a little girl held a cup to catch the blood for making gravy. The duck seemed very contented and when they put him down (the blood all in a cup) he waddled twice and found that he was dead. We ate him later, stuffed and roasted; and many other dishes, with the wine of that year and the year before . . . (pp. 275–76)

The education that makes possible the appreciation of wines is complete. In a changing world and changeable circumstances, Hemingway forged unforeseen alliances. He found the resources to return to all that is permanent in the world of writing and defined his ideal audience, the people of Castille; he found echoes of Walt Whitman's "cavalry crossing a ford" (p. 274), that taps into the primeval forest of all unforgettable writing: "If your memory is good you may ride still through the forest of Irati with the trees like drawing in a child's fairy book" (p. 274). All things runs down, things change, and death is ever present—but not quite. Death is both nemesis and secret ally. The immortals in *Gulliver's Travels* do not know death, nor do they possess memory. Death is made visible in Spain and in Hemingway's writing; in the bullfight, it is there in the strength and ferocity of the bull. For the writer, it is there in the workings of memory. Death clears a space for memory, for precisely the memory created by the living in their cunning response to an always-impending death. Were it not for death and the actions it engenders, on the part of the bullfighter and that of the writer, life—and what makes for life—would be simply and irrevocably forgotten.[19] Everything has a price and facing death, Hemingway tells us, is the price paid for living with feeling. Thanks to a death in the afternoon, as we approach the dusk, we exchange for a single encompassing meaning a present proliferation of vivid images without end:

> Now the essence of the greatest emotional appeal of bullfighting is the feeling of immortality that the bullfighter feels in the middle of a great *faena* and that he gives to the spectators. He is performing a work of art and he is playing with death, bringing it closer, closer, closer, to himself, a death that you know is in the horns because you have the canvas-covered bodies of the horses on the sand to prove it. He gives the feeling of his immortality, and, as you watch it, it becomes yours. Then when it belongs to both of you he proves it with the sword. (p. 213)

Life is a limited asset and there is no reason to doubt a precious asset. Any writer who makes his reader see this possesses an ethic and acknowledges a professional responsibility:

> Let those who want to save the world if you can get to see it clear and as a whole. Then any part you make will represent the whole if it's truly made. The thing to do is to work and learn to make it. (p. 278)

# Chapter IV

# "My Book Has Created Me"

What prudent man would write a single honest word about himself today?

Nietzsche

History, in the march of times, makes the historian much more than that it is made by him. My book has created me. I am its work.

Michelet

1

To be born posthumously is probably the fate of every genuine modern work. As Hemingway writes in *Death in the Afternoon*: "Historians speak highly of all dead bullfighters. To read any history of the great fighters of the past it would seem impossible that they ever had bad days or that the public was ever dissatisfied with them" (p. 240). As revealing is Hemingway's description of Joselito's public reception on the day before his death: "he was hooted, whistled at and had cushions thrown at him the last day he fought in Madrid, the 15th of May, 1920, while he was working his second bull, after having cut the ear of his first, and was hit in the face by a cushion while the crowd shouted '*Que se vaya! Que se vaya!*' which can be translated 'May he get the hell out of here and stay!'" (p. 242).

When *Death in the Afternoon* was published, Hemingway experienced, for the first time, a dramatic shift in his public reception. Arguably one of the most interesting and adventurous American works in the 1930s, and one which distilled Hemingway's private obsession with seeing "things clearly and as a whole," *Death in the Afternoon* was a critical failure. Hemingway's letters of the period reflect his disillusionment. "Haven't seen the reviews except a lengthy poop-on in Times (a man should be pooped on by the Times)," he wrote Dos Passos, "and a condescendentious piece of phony intellectuality by Bob Coates in the New Yorker" (*L*, p. 374). Then, in quick succession, he saw Malcom Cowley's "Will he ever give us, I wonder, his farewell to farewell?"[1]; Mencken's "That Hemingway boy is quite a case;"[2] and, far worse, since Hemingway thought him an ally, Max Eastman's "Why does our iron advocate of straight talk about what things are, our full-sized man, our ferocious realist, go blind and wrap himself up in clouds of juvenile romanticism the moment he crosses the border on his way to the Spanish bullfight?"[3] These reviews reflected in part the new political sensitivities of the 1930s and also a standard critical practice of conflating a writer's evolving production with an earlier and now more understandable thrust of his writing. These facts, however, are secondary to Hemingway's reaction to the reviews of his *tauromaquia*, since the book's reception decisively affected his next works *in themselves*, both their form and subject matter. As a measure of his sensitivity to the attacks on *Death in the Afternoon*, he wrote his editor: "I am tempted never to publish another damned thing. The swine aren't worth writing for. I swear to Christ they're not. Every phase of the whole racket is so disgusting that it makes you feel like vomiting" (*L*, p. 394). As well, his son Gregory remembers "showing him *Ferdinand the Bull*, which I rather liked then. 'That goddam kid's book made ten times more than *Death in the Afternoon*,' he said. 'I worked harder on *Death in the Afternoon* than on any book in my life, and that jerk who wrote Ferdinand might have spent a month on it.'"[4]

A few months later, when preparing the proofs for *Winner Take Nothing* (also badly received, attacked, at one extreme, by the *Saturday Review of Literature*, and, at the other, by *New Masses*), Hemingway recalls his disappointment, "Why write as far as that goes?" and concluded "because I have to" (*L*, p. 401). It is likely that Hemingway knew better than to expect public and critical approval; consider Joselito's fate in his last appearance. Yet, he had made a genuine effort to educate his public and failed. Indeed, the popular tide had turned and he learned, in the process, that his first success was likely based on shaky grounds. When he thought that he had been applying shocks to the system and gaining an audience that shared his concern, he had merely been used by the system, by "power":

> It's damned funny when I used to get the horrors about the way things were going those guys (Cowley, etc.) never took the slightest interest nor even followed it.
>
> They were all in Europe and got worked up over Tristan Tzara when the god damnest things were happening—then when you've gotten as hot about something or as burned up and finally disillusioned on the *working* of anything but intelligent political assassination then they start out and they say, "Don't you see the injustice, the Big Things that are happening. Why don't you write about them, etc." (*L*, p. 374)

Asked to share the unpalatable vinegar of the "grapes of wrath," what was Hemingway to do? Well, as he had done more than once before, shift ground and abnegate the customary role of the author: "Also it is very possible that tearing down is more important than building up" (*L*, p. 375).

Hemingway's situation in the 1930s, beginning with the reception of *Death in the Afternoon*, possessed uncanny similarities to his first years in Paris and his involvement in what Fitzgerald called "cucoo [*sic*] magazines."[5] A new avant-garde had found roots in the New York literary establishment and manifested the typical narrowness of movements, the same self-serving sense of superiority. Throughout the 1930s, Hemingway was nevertheless consistent in his defense of the individual and individual differences as the only basis of a socially valid art. Ideas of class allegiance were obviously anathema to his beliefs, artistic or otherwise. As for his declared strategy of "tearing down," it was directed at critics who so ruinously misunderstood *Death in the Afternoon*, and, consequently, whose judgment could not be trusted to "build up" anything of value. To Ivan Kashkeen, his

Russian translator, Hemingway explained the logic underlying his work: "Every book I have written I try to purify the party and get rid of all the fools who like you or your writing for what you or it are not and the N.Y. critics now hate what I write very strongly but not very efficiently" (*L*, p. 430). We can now modify the assertion with which we began this chapter. If the modern work is born posthumously, this is not an accident, not the result of the artist's passivity in specific contexts. Rather, the modern work resists easy appropriation. As Nietzsche was possibly the first to understand (if not the first, surely the most explicit), the modern author wants to be misunderstood, needs to be mistaken, if he is to accomplish his purpose.

## 2

*Green Hills of Africa* is a book written at mid-career, written at a time when Hemingway well knew his difference as an author and the anachronism he appeared to many of his critics. It is, like *Death in the Afternoon*, the product of self-absorption, but with an important difference. Where *Death in the Afternoon* involves an analysis of the modern aesthetic roots of Hemingway's writing and the production of his singular text, *Green Hills of Africa* is a book that examines the nature of the modern writer's career as an ongoing struggle to produce his text. *Green Hills of Africa* is, indeed, "re-creative," as an examination of a life-long preoccupation with the production of a text. The careers of modern writers and the production of their texts are interconnected, as Said suggests. A text is "a statement of a career fully commanded by neither public pressure (even though that plays a part) nor the ordinary conventions that prescribe a literary vocation. On the contrary, the career is aboriginal; hence its problems."[6] Thus, a possible rationale for "Papa's" first appearance in *Green Hills of Africa*, as Said explains: "In the end, we see that there is an almost annoying resemblance between the author's egoism and the character of his work. Or, to put it differently, there is a real, unavoidable coincidence between an author's egocentricity and the kind of eccentricity found exclusively in his text."[7] Said's analysis derives from a comparative study of a great many modern writers—Wilde, Hopkins, Proust, James, Joyce, and so forth—and, at the very least, it shows that Hemingway's peculiarities are less exceptional when viewed from this perspective. Nevertheless, it is his exceptionalism, perhaps not like Belmonte's, but more along the lines of Joselito and Maera, that he examines in *Green Hills of Africa*.

Questions concerning decadence, fundamental to *Death in the Afternoon*, are not so much set aside in *Green Hills of Africa* as made the basis of a highly particularized and personal reflection. The new work, as always, arises out of the writer's concern with his present circumstances, especially the critical situation of a writer at mid-career, and the unwavering desire expressed at the end of *Death in the Afternoon*: "The thing to do is to work and learn to make it." The feeling that time is short, pressing in on the writer, dominates *Green Hills of Africa*; the possibility of an ongoing work requires dealing with this reality. Essentially "time recaptured," as we see in the literary associations evoked by the hunt, is Hemingway's objective. Given the example of other modern writers, one finds that an individualized search (set out in the manner of a hunt) has a general bearing on the nature of modern art and the modern career. Like Proust, for example, Hemingway has come to understand that a seemingly aimless existence is a modern document of the "work in progress"; and that "literature" is what is made by the passage of time, as it overrides consciously held intentions and ideas. To realize this goal requires time:

> It is not pleasant to have a time limit by which you must get your kudu or perhaps never get it, nor even see one. It is not the way hunting should be. It is too much like these boys who used to be sent to Paris with two years in which to make good as writers or painters after which, if they had not made good, they could go home and into their father's business. The way to hunt is for as long as you live against as long as there is such and such an animal; just as the way to paint is as long as there is you and colors and canvas, and to write as long as you can live and there is pencil and paper and ink or any machine to do it with, or anything you care to write about, and you feel a fool, and you are a fool, to do it any other way. But here we were, now, caught by time . . . being forced into that most exciting perversion of life; the necessity of accomplishing something in less time than should truly be allowed for its doing. (p. 12)

Africa offers yet another chance to bind a life to a work, a meaning to a practice albeit in an eccentric fashion—"that most exciting perversion of life"—but this potential merging is, of necessity, precarious. Africa, similar to so many of the settings for Hemingway's activity, has been overrun by foreigners who are transforming the country. In the narrative of *Green Hills of Africa*, this radical disturbance is announced by Kandisky's noisy arrival, an intrusion that spoils the stalk for kudu at the beginning of the book.

Kandisky is employed by East Indians, who are partly responsible for the present exploitation of Africa. He seems impervious to the implications of his position, perhaps because he delights in the "life of the mind." In any case, he reads and thrives on intellectual discussions; moreover, he recalls Hemingway's name:

> "Hemingway is a name I have heard. Where? Where have I heard it?
> Oh, yes. The *dichter*. You know Hemingway the poet?"
> "Where did you read him?"
> "In the *Querschnitt*." (p. 7)

Later at camp, where they meet again, the two discuss his present circumstances as a writer, and the current conditions of modern writing. Hemingway ends the discussion with an affirmation of his initial goal to produce writing that is "more difficult than poetry. It is a prose that has never been written. But it can be written, without tricks and without cheating. With nothing that will go bad afterwards." And the single, most important requirement is survival and enough time to achieve his goal: "The hardest thing, because time is so short, is for him to survive and get his work done" (p. 27). Kandisky leaves and the reader now sees that "life of the mind" is one thing, life in time, absorbed in a writing career, another.

*Green Hills of Africa* is structured by relationships to time; and, in broad terms, Hemingway's African adventure explores the effects of time and its use and abuse. Epic in structure, if not in its psychological grounding of experience, the book begins "in the middle of things." Part I depicts the hunt's interruption, an unproductive stalk, conversations at the base camp involving impediments to achieving the writer's objective. Part II recalls the author's first arrival in Africa, a period when time was of no consequence, trophies abundant and even the hunter's occasional mistakes a source of fun. With Part III, the interrupted hunt restarts and a first conscious attempt is made to circumvent the feeling that "time is short." This section ends in failure. The last part of *Green Hills of Africa*, "Pursuit as Happiness," achieves its objective, in overcoming time, but its success is also somewhat mitigated. At the very end of the book, Hemingway describes the scene that led in part to his determination to write *Green Hills of Africa*, and the basis of a success that does not entirely depend on the hunt, in itself:

> The hills made shadows on the water, which was flat calm and rather stagnant looking. There were many grebes, making spreading wakes in the water as they swam, and I was counting them and wondering why they were never mentioned in the Bible. I decided that those people were not naturalists.
>
> "I'm not going to walk on it," Karl said, looking at the dreary lake; "It's been done already."
>
> "You know," P. O. M. said, "I can't remember Mr. J. P.'s face. . . . He isn't the way he looks in a photograph. In a little while I won't be able to remember him at all. Already I can't see him."
>
> "You must remember him," Karl said to her.
>
> "I can remember him," I said. "I'll write you a piece some time and put him in." (pp. 294–95)

Generally, *Green Hills of Africa* is a naturalist's handbook and its "memory" a secularized version of religious conviction every bit as difficult as "walking on water." The modern work must now accomplish what was done in the past based on faith. (Again, Mungo Park has no direct bearing on the book that followed *Death in the Afternoon*.) Faithful to experience, where "Mr. J. P." is a part of the whole, Hemingway imagines a kind of writing in which nothing "will go bad afterwards," where the naturalist's faith does not lead to disillusionment.

According to Edmund Wilson, Hemingway had "an acute sense of the cost and danger of doing anything worth doing,"[8] a sense that is undoubtedly more acute when "time is short." At mid-career, Hemingway observes, "something happens to our good writers" (p. 19). In the following passage, he is discussing his contemporaries, but his observations are as easily applied to himself:

> They have to write to keep up their establishment, their wives, and so on, and they write slop. It is not slop on purpose but because it is hurried. Because they write when there is nothing to say or no water in the well.
>
> Because they are ambitious. Then, once they have betrayed themselves, they justify it with more slop. Or else they read the critics. If they believe the critics when they say they are great then they must believe them when they say they are rotten and they lose confidence. (p. 23)

External circumstances are a particular danger "at a certain age," and unfortunately, their effects felt only after the damage is done. Equally, an author's writing registers the signs of slop or the simple absence of a work. In either case, the time-limit now at play in their career has been ignored and the "popular" or public time that responds to the writer's "establishment" or critical fashions obscures the intrinsic temporal logic of the work and career. Both forms of badly used time are destructive to the writer, who becomes defensive or paralyzed by guilt and self-condemnation.

Hemingway's analysis is in no sense gratuitous, since while hunting, he, too, oscillates between days of remarkable facility, which produce mere "slop," and other days that are dispiriting because nothing seems to work. He runs a gamut of emotions, from defensiveness to lack of confidence. Indeed, Hemingway's self-portrait (caricature?) under these circumstances is not attractive or amusing. Importantly, though, his emotional extremes are measured by the practice of the hunt, in which self-destructive tendencies are overcome as he finds a new orientation as hunter. Hemingway has experienced the malaise that occurs "to our good writers at a certain age," and he is attracted to Africa in the hope of recapturing his inaugural ideal of writing, which existed before he achieved popularity and a degree of financial success, before the inadvertent and twin creation of a public personality and an invisible or disguised craftsman. This divided self corresponds to a life's work that has lost its course. Africa, consequently, stands for the zone of writing and productivity that either precedes the divisions that arise at a certain age or that follows the questioning of direction at mid-career.

Hemingway sets out his naturalist's viewpoint both in terms of the state of writing in the mid-1930s and in terms of a tradition of American writing that dates from those classics "who wrote like exiled colonials from an England of which they were never a part to a newer England that they were making" (p. 20). "Emerson, Whittier, and Company" are pushed aside because of their failure to break their ties to an historical development that was not properly theirs as American writers. "They had minds, yes. Nice, dry, clean minds," Hemingway writes, reminding us of Kandisky's exiled state and his enjoyment of the "life of the mind," but they had no life in time, the particular time that allowed them the opportunity to assert their heritage as Americans. As well, the classic American tradition accepted history *tout court*, as an inevitable pattern of development that coincides with colonial exploitation. Against this literature of exile, Hemingway sets out a loose grouping of American naturalists, whose only creed is based on the need to stand apart, rejecting the lure of an English patrimony. In this context, Hemingway locates a liberating perception as the basis for a radically altered view of the work of art. Now he states his admiration for *Huckleberry Finn*, the beginning of an indigenous American tradition: "All American writing comes from that. There was nothing before. There has been nothing as good since" (p. 22).

A child's book and, more broadly, a book concerned with the possibility of fresh beginnings of the sort that belong to the partially liberated "youth" of the American frontier, *Huckleberry Finn* explores the problems encountered when trying to disentangle the specifically American experience from colonial convictions and behavior. Huck's disguises are his way of outwitting the still active obstacle of an older mentality. At first, Huck adopts disguises for protection, but they quickly lead to more confusion and uncertainty. Huck does try to enact the lessons of an older, dominant culture, but the process wears thin—so that through ridiculous encounters, often accompanied by violence, he comes to recognize the deeper nature of his bondage and starts to appreciate his brotherhood with Jim. Jim's more visible oppression is a counterpart to Huck's subjection to alien values and the need to pattern himself, as part of a liberating game, on the "ideal" of the model culture. Huck's tactic, his education, and his particular American "genius," recall the description of Belmonte's revolution in *Death in the Afternoon*, in his transformation of preexisting, limiting circumstances into a source of liberation and basis for his particular form of expression.

*Green Hills of Africa* is a partial testimony to the living force of Mark Twain's masterpiece. It begins where *Huckleberry Finn* stopped, in a new land that has yet to experience the full impact of colonization. Hemingway, too, adopts disguises in his book, the main disguise being his role as hunter, in order to realize his steady purpose. The hunt, in short, outlines a career at a certain point: "an absolutely true book" that "competes with a work of the imagination," as stated in the foreword to *Green Hills of Africa*. Similar to writing, which no longer seems a "serious occupation," the hunt is known for its impracticality, but for this reason it can be opposed to the progress and practicality introduced by outsiders to Africa and to the hunt. The lack of progress in the hunt is, in fact, a crucial component of its long-range usefulness and meaning. Progress, such as an outsider's purposeful exploitation of Africa, is ultimately self-defeating for all concerned:

> A continent ages quickly once we come. The natives live in harmony with it. But the foreigner destroys, cuts down the trees, drains the water, so that the water supply is altered and in a short time the soil, once the sod is turned under, is cropped out and, next, it starts to blow away as it has blown away in every old country and as I had seen it start to blow in Canada. The earth gets tired of being exploited. A country wears out quickly unless man puts back in it his residue and that of all his beasts. When he quits using beasts and uses machines, he earth defeats him quickly. . . . A country was made to be found as we found it. We are the intruders and after we are dead we may have ruined it but it will still be there and we don't know what the next changes are. I suppose they all end up like Mongolia. (pp. 284–85)

Published in 1935, these observations undoubtedly had resonance and, although Hemingway does not directly address specific political issues, the passage is alive to an understanding of class interests. Who, after all, gains in the short run from exploitation of the land? Characteristically, Hemingway expands his reflection by asserting the activity of writing as paradigmatic of productive activity: "I would come back to Africa but not to make a living from it. I could do that with two pencils and a few hundred sheets of the cheapest paper. But I would come back to where it pleased me to live; to really live. Not just let my life pass." At the end of *Green Hills of Africa*, we find yet

another evocation of the conditions that abetted Hemingway's beginnings as writer, but now his practice is felt to extend to a mode of life.
Writing has for its goal an activity where "nothing will go bad afterwards," a form of productive husbanding and a certain relationship
to a country. The vitality of writing and of the writers' careers depend
on their being seen as ends in themselves, as possessing their own
demands and internal logic and time frame. This belief is made the
basis of numerous object lessons in *Green Hills of Africa*. Hemingway
repeatedly depicts an act as it happens, and from which it gains whatever value it has—sensation, experience, and essence—and, through
repetition, the same act as understood, or, rather, misunderstood from
the outside or at a later time. At the end of Part I of the book, for
instance, Hemingway sets out the confusion that surrounds the
shooting of a lion, a kill erroneously credited—after the event—to his
wife: "*Hey la Mama! huh! huh! huh! Hey la Mama! huh! huh! huh!*"
(p. 42). Seen from the outside and in terms of its aftermath, an act
loses its value. Playing a role equally defeats the desire that "nothing
will go bad afterwards," as we see in the farcical example of Garrick,
the hated native guide labeled "the theatrical one" (p. 2). Garrick's
silliness concerns his adopting a Western role and "acting" according
to his perception of Western standards. Thus, Hemingway farcically
imagines Garrick in the movies, a perfect medium, in his view, for the
silliness of repetition: "Tell him I'll put him in the cinema. Got a part
for him. Little thing I thought up on the way home. It may not work
but I like the plot. Othello or the Moor of Venice. D'you like it? It's
got a wonderful idea. You see this jig we call Othello falls in love with
a white girl who's never been around at all so we call her Desdemona.
Like it? They've been after me to write it for years but I drew the color
line" (p. 166). The nature of an act and its reenactment is central to
Hemingway's preoccupations in *Green Hills of Africa*. Repetitions
from the outside, like that of the critic who re-presents modern
writing for others or that of "classic" American writers who wanted
to make "a newer England," leads to the erasure of intrinsic values.
Failure is an inevitable product of repetition and the adoption of standards not intrinsic to a specific action or location. Hemingway's
response is often a crude caricature of the failed repetition.

The hunt, understood as a whole and integral action, portrays
Hemingway as something of a failure in comparison to Karl, his

hunting companion. Here, the pattern involves first showing Hemingway's exultation at the kill followed by his deflation when, back at camp, he is shown Karl's larger trophies. A parallel situation is that of the exultant writer in the act of writing, and *after*. Hemingway's adventure ends with an especially depressing event, as he returns to camp with two impressive kudu trophies only to learn that Karl's (who never left the proximity of the base camp) are larger and more impressive. This aspect of the hunt is, indeed, unnerving, more so, in fact, than any external interference. As "Mr. J. P." tells the author: "We have very primitive emotions. . . . It's impossible not to be competitive. Spoils everything though" (p. 293). The act of writing, consequently, lies between the two extremes of primitive emotions and the hypersensitivity of acculturated feelings. Nevertheless, Hemingway's "absolutely true book" sets out his recognition of his self-absorption and how certain aspects of career distort social relationships. More basic to the work is the modernist tenet of impersonality:

> If you serve time for society, democracy, and other things quite young, and declining further enlistment make yourself responsible only to yourself, you exchange the pleasant, comforting stench of comrades for something you can never feel in any other way than by yourself. That something I cannot yet define completely but the feeling comes when you write well and truly of something and know impersonally that you have written in that way . . . (pp. 148–49)

Clearly, competition has no value in an action that is known impersonally, nor has it any meaning in the context of an experience that Hemingway tracks in the subsequent and arresting metaphor of the stream,

> that you are living with, knowing, learning about, and loving, (that) has moved, as it moves, since before man, and that it has gone by the shoreline of that long, unhappy island since before Columbus sighted it and the things you find out about it, and those that have lived in it are permanent and of value because that stream will flow, as it has flowed. . . .

The stream is profoundly indifferent to human striving, to cultural aims, to individual preferences and quirks of personality. It is a movement, a form of comprehension and of permanence:

after the Indians, after the Spaniards, after the British, after the
Americans and all the Cubans and all the systems of governments,
the richness, the poverty, the martyrdom, the sacrifice and the
venality and the cruelty are all gone as the high-piled scow of
garbage, bright-colored, white-flecked, ill-smelling, now tilted on its
side, spills off its load into the blue water . . . (p. 149)

The aftermath of civilizations and its detritus belong to the
"garbage pickers who pluck their prizes with long poles, as interested,
as intelligent, and as accurate as historians: they have the viewpoint"
(p. 150). Significantly, historians border the stream and highlight the
centrality of those who "live in it"; and, consistent with their role,
they focus on the residue of human effort and desire: "the flotsam of
palm fronds, corks, bottles, and used electric light globes, seasoned
with an occasional condom or a deep floating corset, the torn leaves
of a student's exercise book, a well-inflated dog, the occasional rat,
the no-longer distinguished cat" (p. 149). For Hemingway, it is a
question of perspective and of differentiating the spoils that attract
the historian from the object of true writing. If writing is more
truthful than the accumulation of dead facts by the historian, it is
because it is the difficult movement toward a permanence—which
does not "go bad afterwards"—that, in turn, uncovers the freshness
of all individual voices that strive against the unstable generality of
peoples, systems of government, and critical fashions.

Being the reiterated striving of a solitary writing activity, the
stream offers a renewed perspective within the surfeit of individual
lives and exhausted cultures. More obliquely, the stream reestablishes
the communality of writers as seemingly different as Hemingway and
Joyce: "And that last night, drunk, with Joyce and the thing he kept
quoting from Edgar Quinet, 'Fraiche et rose comme au jour de la
bataille.' I didn't have it right I knew. And when you saw him he
would take up a conversation interrupted three years before" (p. 71).
The stream flows from one year and one generation to the next. It
newly awaits the writer each day, "fraiche et rose." Also, a battle
awaits him who intends to overcome the restraint and interruptions
that work against the freeing of writing "fraiche et rose." Hemingway
"didn't have it right,"[9] but this is of less importance than his rein-
scription of Joyce's meaning within the state of his present career, as

he perceived it. Time erases much that seems valuable and Hemingway's desire for permanence sets aside a static reality for a tradition (and thus his career) that is constantly in the process of being made, and remade. There is the tangible pathos of all things in the process of disappearing, but also the permanence of the "real," as he conceived it: "I was thinking how real that Russia of the time of our Civil War was, as real as any other place, as Michigan, or the prairie north of town and the woods around Evan's farm, of how, through Turgenieff, I knew I had lived there" (p. 108). More generally, Hemingway writes: "we have been there in the books and out of the books—and where we go, if we are any good, there you can go as we have been" (p. 109).

Hemingway's reflections on the "stream" recall Walter Benjamin's insightful essay "The Destructive Character." In it, Benjamin observes that there exist two ways to pass things on to posterity: by making the past "untouchable" and thus "conserving" it, or by making it "practicable" and thus "liquidating" it. A product of an earlier religious apprehension of the sacred, the former attitude corresponds to the monumental history derided by Nietzsche; whereas, the naturalist's perspective, given as Hemingway's orientation at the beginning and end of *Green Hills of Africa*, concerns the ongoing engagements and experimentation that test tradition. In general terms, Hemingway's position as writer involves testing cultural wisdom through concrete and present struggles, determining what works for him as a writer with particular objectives, and, consequently, transforming tradition to "the liquid state."[10] The physicality of the hunt is crucial to Hemingway because it tests in a practical fashion an activity that warrants preservation.

A suggestive approach to the striking image of the stream, and the concept of artistic permanence, can be found in Said's analysis of Proust and Joyce—among many other modern writers—and their orientation toward their literary careers. Proust, in particular, serves as a clear example of the central importance of "vocation" to the modern writer and of his obsession with creating a book that achieves the permanence of the work of art. It is well known that Hemingway often referred to Proust in the 1940s as an influence when he began writing the novels that were finally published after his death, but there are also references to Proust in his letters from a much earlier time. For all that, their preoccupations are strikingly similar and bear examination. The last volume of *In Search of Lost Time*, "Time Regained," focuses on the permanence, "the essence," found in the work of art, while Hemingway addresses the same issue in his more condensed "naturalist" style, but, as Said says of Proust, they have this in common: "a contrast is sustained between his empirical self, exposed to interior and exterior dangers and his artistic self, whose creation he intends as an ultimate replacement for the loss of memory, will, and existence in his empirical self. What is common to both selves is the idea of death, which (Proust) says *"me tenait une compagnie aussi incessante que l'idee du moi."* Proust's goal is "to write so that there will be no discontinuity between in the world of past time he has inhabited and now carries within him in order to transcribe it."[11] This is the basis of a "past recaptured" in Proust and also in Hemingway for whom, "if we are any good, there you can go as we have been." The key to this "true" recovery is a physical sensation that triggers a vivid memory of an event and that gives "the impression of an essence outside of time." Outside of time, a work of literature "does not go bad" in the passage and decay of time. A rejected passage in the manuscript version of *Green Hills of Africa* (where Hemingway discusses his father's suicide) ends with this assertion:

> Now, truly, in actual danger, I felt a clean feeling as in a shower. Of course it was easy now. That was because I no longer cared what happened. I knew it was better to live it so that if you died you had done everything that you could do about your work and your enjoyment of life up to that minute, reconciling the two, which is very difficult.[12]

The similarities between Proust and Hemingway do not extend to the "elaborate" analysis of writing in Proust's "Time Regained." But their common concerns are unmistakable.

As suggested above, *Green Hills of Africa* was a reactive work in its conception, reactive to his critical reception but also reactive to his perception of what had become of his career. It locates a more essential foundation for writing in the complicated temporality of the stream, one which recasts the writer's relationship to time, in the separateness of writing, and to his career. In this context, it is possible to see that the mitigated failures of *Green Hills of Africa* are the result of personal limitations and external accidents and that the disputed value of trophies are meant to underscore the more basic reality of the hunt and career as ongoing processes. If properly conducted, the hunt should be fully consuming:

> But that damned sable bull. I should have killed him; but it was a running shot. To hit him at all I had to use him all as target. Yes, you bastard, but what about the cow you missed twice, prone, standing broadside? Was that a running shot? No. If I'd gone to bed last night I would not have done that. Or if I'd wiped out the bore to get the oil out she would not have thrown high the first time. Then I would not have pulled down and shot under her the second shot. Every damned thing is your fault if you're any good. (p. 281)

Mistakes result from the absence of absolute commitment. Similarly, in "Pursuit Remembered," which contains an extended reverie of Hemingway's Paris years, quirks of development and idiosyncrasies have value only if channeled into a work, if a writer can get beyond what his life and times have made of him: "Writers are forged in injustice as a sword is forged."

A lull in the hunt and a reading of Tolstoi's *Sevastopol* trigger a series of connected reminiscences: "Then Sevastopol made me think of the Boulevard Sevastopol in Paris, about riding a bicycle down it in the rain on the way home from Strassburg and the slipperiness of the rails of the tram cars and the feeling of riding on greasy, slippery asphalt and cobble in the rain." The writer's emergence is precarious and requires the utmost concentration. Even Hemingway's subsequent description of his "home" is charged with the "slipperiness" of his situation. The passage in question literally underlines the forces at play in the act of writing:

> upstairs of the pavilion in the Notre Dame des Champs in the court-yard with the sawmill (*and the sudden whine of the saw, the smell of sawdust and the chestnut tree over the roof with a mad woman downstairs*) and the year worrying about money . . . (p. 70)

A tenuous balance is struck between, on the one hand, poverty and the threat of madness, and, on the other, work, production, and physical sensations. This is Hemingway's earliest period of rejection and solitary work: "(*all of the stories back in the mail that came in through a slit in the saw-mill door, with notes of rejection that would never call them stories, but always anecdotes, sketches, contes, etc. They did not want them, and we lived on poireaux and drank cahors and water*)." But an ideal sustains his work as seen in the image he now invokes of the fountains at the Place de l'Observatoire:

> (*water sheen rippling on the bronze of horses' manes, bronze breasts and shoulders, green under the thin-flowing water*) and when they put the bust of Flaubert in the Luxembourg on the short cut through the gardens on the way to the rue Soufflot (*one that we believed in, loved without criticism, heavy now in stone as an idol should be*). (p. 71)

Not only is Flaubert "the short cut through the gardens" of newly discovered writing, but he is also the goal of completed writing, commemorated "*in stone as an idol should be*." Other writers are introduced (Stendhal, Dostoyevsky, and Joyce) in the anonymity of the stream, as a function of a process that transforms personal experience into an "essence" of recaptured experience, "*Fraiche et rose comme au jour de la bataille*." Finally, Hemingway returns to his preoccupation with time, the recaptured past and the overcoming of the negative effects of time:

> Now, looking out of the tunnel of trees over the ravine at the sky with white clouds moving across in the wind, I loved the country so that I was happy as you are after you have been with a woman that you really love, when, empty, you feel it welling up again and there it is and you can never have it all and yet what there is, now, you can have, and you want more and more to have and be, and live in, to possess now again for always, for that long, sudden-ended always; making time stand still, sometimes so very still that afterwards you wait to hear it move, and it is slow in starting. (p. 72)

This naturalist description could serve as an emblem of Hemingway's writing, his way of stopping time in order to overcome his duality in time.

*Green Hills of Africa* ends with yet another reverie. Returning to camp after hunting greater kudu, Hemingway recalls an early friend-ship with Captain Dorman-Smith: "what bloody literary discussion we had then; we were literary as hell after the war" (p. 280). He returns from the land of the Masai ("there were no old people" [p. 280]) and it strikes him that he could live happily as a writer in Africa, and, then, there appears an apotheosis of his African adventure when "suddenly, all the trees were full of white storks" (p. 287). Back in camp, Hemingway sees Karl's kudu trophies, and his African adven-ture ends with the anticlimax of a "finished product." Pop advises him: "you always remembers how you shot them. That's what you really get out of it" (p. 287); and explains the meaning of the ritual handshakes of his guides after returning to camp after the hunt for kudu and sable, as "on the order of blood brotherhood but a little less formal." The indirect goal of the hunt, time recaptured, underlies a newly discovered relationship with an appreciative audience, the native guides who participated in the hunt. Of significance, M'Cola, the head guide, is shown to be a better hunter than the author: "I had always sworn to Pop that I could out-track M'Cola but I realized now that in the past I had been giving a sort of Garrick (the despised assis-tant guide) performance . . . I knew M'Cola was immeasurably the better man and the better tracker, Have to tell Pop, I thought" (p. 269). That M'Cola observes and is keenly involved in Hemingway's hunt, that M'Cola participates in the ritual of "blood brotherhood"—this is, for Hemingway, genuine audience acceptance from an informed and different audience, not "angleworms in a bottle."

## 3

Hemingway's African scene involves a prose "more difficult than poetry," perhaps something like a prose of the world that arises from direct experience of a country and that is capable of making endlessly productive correspondences. But as an activity characterized as "this silliness of kudu," or found in literary reveries, the prose of the world also indicates Hemingway's disengagement from current literary prac-tices, the anachronism of his work of recovery in a period of "progress." Proust, in the famous passages of "Time Regained," addresses the concerns that have been discussed in *Green Hills of*

*Africa*. He speaks of the subterranean feat of self-discovery: "What we have not had to decipher, to elucidate by our own efforts, what was clear before we looked at it, is not ours. From ourselves comes only that which we drag forth from obscurity which lies within us, that which to others is unknown." "But this discovery," Proust continues, "which art obliges us to make, is it not, I thought, really the discovery of what, though it ought to be more precious to us than anything in the world, yet remains ordinarily for ever unknown to us, the discovery of our true life, of reality as we have felt it to be . . ." He quickly follows these thoughts with a rejection of the "falseness of so-called realist art," which, through habit, we take to be "reality itself." Particularly decisive, as it reflects on Hemingway's own thoughts:

> I began to perceive that I should not have to trouble myself with the various literary theories which at moments perplexed me—notably those which practitioners of criticism had developed at the time of the Dreyfus case and had taken up again during the war, according to which "the artist must be made to leave his ivory tower" and the themes chosen by the writer ought to be not frivolous or sentimental but rather such things as great working-class movements . . .

Presented parenthetically, the next observation might have found a presence in the "naturalist" debates of *Death in the Afternoon*: "And as to the choice of theme, a frivolous theme will serve as well as a serious for the study of the laws of character, in the same way that a prosecutor can study the laws of anatomy as well in the body of an imbecile as in that of a man of talent, since the great moral laws, like the laws of the circulation of the blood or of renal elimination, vary scarcely at all with the intellectual merit of individuals." One final thought from Proust, to be read, perhaps, with M'Cola in mind:

> The idea of a popular art, like that of a patriotic art, if not actually dangerous seemed to me ridiculous. If the intention was to make art accessible to the people by sacrificing refinements of form, on the ground that they are "all right for the idle rich" but not for anybody else, I had seen enough of fashionable society to know that it is there that one finds real illiteracy and not, let us say, among electricians.[13]

Two very different writers—Hemingway and Proust—resolve similar problems, an art that recaptures experience as lived ("our true life"), a rejection of the "theories" that perplexed, especially as they involve the "major themes" of their time, and the question of audience (if they are to have one).

When it is a matter of public expectations, Hemingway, in any event, saw himself as an outlaw. He wrote to Owen Wister in the late 1920s: "All we can do to restore the old language—as it is spoken it should be written or it dies—is to the good. What if you become an outlaw? I'm afraid we are anyway. We should be maybe" (*L*, p. 301). The hunt, of course, is one of the forms taken by the oldest language and it establishes a bond between Hemingway and his guides: "you ask how this was discussed, worked out, and understood with the bar of language, and I say it was as freely discussed and clearly understood as though we were a cavalry patrol all speaking the same language. We were all hunters except, possibly, Garrick, and the whole thing could be worked out, understood, and agreed to without using anything but a forefinger to signal and a hand to caution" (p. 251). A similar attitude informs Hemingway's political sense of his writing: "A writer is an outlyer like a Gypsy. He can be class conscious only if his talent is limited. If he has enough talent all classes are his province. He takes from them all and what he gives is everybody's property" (*L*, p. 419). The writing that was to follow in the 1930s further explores these perceptions, with the publication of *The First Forty-Nine Stories*, which included four stories that had not been published earlier, *To Have and Have Not* (a "proletariat" novel), and *For Whom the Bell Tolls*, with its guerrilla warfare, love interest, and "political theory."

*Part Three*

# "Now There Is Politics Too"

# Chapter V

# Being Collected

*You know all there is to strategy is*
*to always be strong—and then*
*always to be strong at the right place.*

*Never think that one story represents*
*my viewpoint because it is much too*
*complicated for that.*

Hemingway, Letters

1

*T*he 1930s saw the devaluation of writing as an end in itself. Hemingway was advised to "express" his commitment to external causes, to curb his obsession and transform his writing into a serviceable instrument for "The Big Things that are happening." It was a period of commentary and public causes, the appearance of the *New Masses, Commentary*, and *Partisan Review*. A new, more vocal audience was created, new "institutions of dissemination, preservation, and judgment."[1] Other magazine outlets existed, of course; *Life Magazine* and *Collier's* are two of the better examples that made use of Hemingway's writing. At a later time, academic critics would enter the scene and add yet new layers of complication. None of these mechanisms of reception left Hemingway untouched; they acted as constraints, limiting the work he had planned. Their effect touches on the three closely related aspects of his particular individuality as a writer. The demands of a new critical audience were inhibiting to Hemingway's sense of self at mid-career. As Said explains: "The writer's life, his career, and his text form a system of relationships whose configuration *in real human time* becomes progressively stronger (i.e., more distinct, more individualized and exacerbated). In fact, these relationships gradually become the writer's all-encompassing subject."[2] The Hemingway myth, the larger-than-life "Papa," points to the "system of relationships" outlined by Said, but it is also an image that contests the perspective afforded by new critical circumstances.

From *Winner Take Nothing* through *For Whom the Bell Tolls*, Hemingway directly responded to the attacks of his critics, and in these works disputed their critical assumptions. The next chapter, concerned with *For Whom the Bell Tolls*, explores the question of thought and knowledge, specifically a form of reason found in the Marxist dialectic that seeks to overcome the "unreason" of individual experience. In that context, Robert Jordan is presented as a professor whose serious education begins with his involvement with Pablo's guerrilla group. Hemingway's major works of the 1930s involve educating his public and, as importantly, concern his view of the nature of thought and knowledge. The emphasis, of course, is on their relation to the work of art and the embodied thought found in certain kinds of literature.

As background it should be noted that criticism, in its period of ascendancy, destroyed many writers; Hemingway recorded its threat in *Green Hills of Africa*, as a by-product of modernism and the source of the impotence of his contemporaries. Fitzgerald served as an object lesson for what "happens to our good writers at a certain age" and in the age of critics. Particularly disturbing was Fitzgerald's capitulation in "The Crack Up," the three-part essay first published in *Esquire*:

> Feel awfully about Scott. I tried to write him once (wrote him several times) to cheer him up but he seems to almost take pride in his shamelessness of defeat. The Esquire pieces seem to me to be so miserable. There is another one coming too. I always knew he couldn't

think—he never could—but he had a marvelous talent and the thing
is to use it—not whine in public. Good God, people go through . . .
that emptiness many times in life and come out and do work. . . .
The minute he felt youth going he was frightened again and thought
there was nothing between youth and age. But it is so damned easy
to criticize our friends and I shouldn't write this. I wish we could
help him. (*L*, pp. 437–38)

Nor did Hemingway admire *The Last Tycoon*, in which the description of Stahr (Irving Thalberg) showed that Fitzgerald "still had the technique and the romance of doing anything" but where it could never have been completed "with that gigantic, preposterous outline of how it was to be" (*L*, p. 527). Far more caustic was Hemingway's judgment ten years later: "The Last Tycoon, after the part that is written, and was as far as he could write, is really only a scheme to borrow money on" (*L*, p. 695). These remarks are more than a statement of disillusionment with Fitzgerald. They clarify the basis of Fitzgerald's impotence and his increasing inability to finish any work after the success of *The Great Gatsby*. "At present we have two good writers who cannot write because they have lost confidence through reading critics. If they wrote, sometimes it would be good and sometimes it would be quite bad, but the good would get out. But they have read the critics and they must write masterpieces. The masterpieces the critics said they wrote. They weren't masterpieces, of course. They were just quite good books. So now they cannot write at all. The critics have made them impotent" (*GHA*, pp. 23–24). Concerning *The Last Tycoon*, "with that gigantic, preposterous outline," it confirmed for Hemingway that Fitzgerald was continuing to please the critics, by incorporating the fashionable preoccupations of the late 1930s—with Marxist union organizers, capitalist corruption, and so forth.

About the same time "The Crack Up" was published and in contrast to Fitzgerald, Hemingway began to lay plans for *The First Forty-Nine Stories*. This collection would include the new stories he had written since *Winner Take Nothing*, some of which had been published in *Esquire*. He worried that if published separately in a new collection, the critics "will jump on them one at a time. Ignore one and pan the other." Consequently, Hemingway would meet them on his own ground, by publishing a retrospective collection of all his stories, which would be "too big for them, too damn impressive." As Hemingway goes on to say:

> I don't think it is persecution mania or egotism if I say that there are a lot of critics who really seem to hate me very much and would like to put me out of business. And I don't think I mean it conceitedly when I say that a lot of it is jealousy; I do what they are afraid to do; and they hate you for it. Now there is politics too. So I think the best thing to do is to make a book with so much good reading, and so obviously good that you have them on quality and bulk anyway.
>
> What do you think? (*L*, p. 471)

In traditional terms, "quality and bulk" stand for the status and the volume of a work. Status typically concerns a work's reception, reputation, and earning power, while volume refers to the ever-expanding text, the "life's work." As they apply to Hemingway and to his predecessors and contemporaries, these categories were redefined in the modern period: "volume, in the cases of Mallarmé, Hopkins, Eliot, Joyce, Valery, Kafka, and Wilde has to do with density, rarity and irregularity. Status has to do with the text's inaccessibility to the 'ordinary' public and concomitantly, with its extraordinary capacity for being with, or being part of, other literature."[3] Given these considerations, "The Snows of Kilimanjaro," one of the new stories that begins the collection, is especially important (as argued below). Arguably, it is an addition to the work's "volume" by virtue of the fact that it is a further movement of "meaning fulfillment"[4] as underlying the logic of career, while it maintains the work's "status" as a "difficult" story because of its relation to other literature.

The "bulk" of accomplished work was intended as a challenge to Hemingway's critics, an incentive for reassessment, but, more essential, it is a statement of an internal reality—the writer's ongoing commitment at mid-career. The preface that introduces the collection of stories may have been written as a contrast to "The Crack Up." Unlike Fitzgerald's recantation, the preface is short and impersonal. Implicitly, it acknowledges "that emptiness" that people go through "many times in life," but it is more alive to its positive implications: "and come out and do work." Thus, the preface does not suggest a progress over time, but the repeated overcoming of negative circumstances and the value of work that is a constant recovery of purpose. Moreover, individual stories are said to be the product of time and place, local, specific, and changing, some good and others "not so good." As a concession to the reader, Hemingway says: "There are many different kinds of stories in this book. I hope you will find some that you like." He then gives a short list of stories he still enjoys and has had to disown, "those that have now achieved some notoriety so that school teachers include them in story collections that their pupils have to buy in story courses, and you are always embarrassed to read them and wonder whether you really wrote them or did you maybe hear them somewhere." The falsification that he reacts to is of two kinds: the transformation of personal individualized activity into either a technical lesson or into a form of abstract and impersonal understanding residing in the public domain. Hemingway concludes his preface with his perspective on the relationship of a writer's life to his work:

> In going where you have to go, and doing what you have to do, and seeing what you have to see, you dull and blunt the instrument you write with. But I would rather have it bent and dull and know I had put on the grindstone again and hammer it into shape and put a whetstone to it, and know that I had something to write about, than to have it bright and shining and nothing to say, or smooth and well-oiled in the closet, but unused.

Pragmatic and low-key, Hemingway's preface is subordinated to his stories, which are themselves ruled by chance and altered circumstances, "in going where you have to go . . ." As well, the stories are an effective instrument for conveying Hemingway's perception of his present circumstances, of his "life as lived," beginning with *In Our Time* on through the four new stories that introduce his collection: "The Short Happy Life of Francis Macomber," "The Capital of the World," "The Snows of Kilimanjaro," and "Old Man at the Bridge."

In the new stories that begin Hemingway's collection, chance and attending risks dominate as the circumstance for any action. By chance, Francis Macomber finds a way to momentarily assert his manhood. In the same way, Harry in "The Snows of Kilimanjaro" is forced to a reckoning: "I don't see why that had to happen to your leg. What have we done to have that happen to us" (p. 55). Nothing had meant very much until "a thorn had scratched his knee as they moved forward trying to photograph a herd of waterbuck" (p. 62). Before this, "you spoke only from habit and to be comfortable" (p. 59). By chance, the unnamed old man in "Old Man at the Bridge" is dispossessed in a Spanish offensive. Then, there is Paco, in "The Capital of the World," killed by chance and miscalculation, and "he had not even had time to be disappointed in the Garbo picture which disappointed all Madrid for a week" (p. 51). Chance and unaccountable errors may be the basis of disillusionment but they are also the source of a positive reconstruction, paradoxically the only "safe" ground of permanence. In all of Hemingway's "clean well lighted places," one sees the irrefutable *fatum* of experience, against which a certain clarity is introduced. The slant of light, a metaphor for Hemingway's perspective, necessarily entails a system of injustice, affirmations and negations from a specific and finite point of view.

If modern conditions are ignoble and if the finest feelings are linked to decadence, then an act that tries to reestablish nobility will appear brutish. In *Genealogy of Morals*, Nietzsche observed the modern need, the curative necessity of the "blond beast of prey," as well as the violence directed at the "effeminacy" of modern pity, fellow understanding, and Christian virtue, as a way of blocking a reactive conscience, *"ressentiment."*[5] This informs Francis Macomber's rejection of his wife—and with it the guilt he experienced in her presence—as it does the callousness of Harry's treatment of Helen. More explicitly, Hemingway identifies his protagonists with actual beasts of prey. In his death, Harry flies to the top of Kilimanjaro, where he is awaited by the solitary carcass of a "dried and frozen" leopard; and Francis Macomber, who had earlier been kept awake by his terror of facing a lion the next morning, dies in a movement that identifies him with a charging water buffalo:

> aiming carefully, (he) shot again with the buffalo's huge bulk almost on him and his rifle almost level with the oncoming head, nose out, and he could see the little eyes and the head started to lower and he felt a sudden white-hot, blinding flash explode inside his head and that was all he ever felt. (pp. 35–36)

The cost of nobility is nothing less than total risk, at the limit of what one can be; and the product of a successful action, to say the least, is bizarre. It is easier, perhaps, to side with the wives in these stories, whose reaction to their husbands' deaths is "crying hysterically."

It is tempting to imagine Fitzgerald's "Crack Up" from Hemingway's point of view as an expression of "effeminacy," where brutality is the antidote, from a superficial standpoint, for "whining in public." But brutality is essential to the completion of a work, since it is, in the words of Paul de Man in *Blindness and Insight*, the manifestation of the modernist tenet that supports "the right of what is coming into being because of one's own actions."[6] The absence of a work and betrayal of talent in Harry's case coincide with his accommodation to his wife's ethos. When he recognizes his imminent death, he turns cruel, attacks her pitilessly: "It's trying to kill to keep yourself alive" (p. 58). Cruelty is an index of his work's autonomy; it severs sentimental ties that swamp (in tears) the accomplishment of the work, erects a barrier between the writer and a grasping public so that the work arises through indirection: "So this is how you died, in whispers that you did not hear." As Harry dies, the work he intended to write is written and it is written against his impending death. The recovery of his youthful aspirations conditions his subject matter as writer, common events of a "life as lived." And all the while, vultures and hyenas, attracted by his gangrenous leg, move closer: "three of the birds squatted obscenely" (p. 52) and "it came with a rush; not a rush of water nor of wind; but of a sudden evil-smelling emptiness and the odd thing was that the hyena slipped lightly along the edge of it" (p. 64). In time, death "simply occupied space . . . and it crouched now, heavier, so he could not breathe" (pp. 74–75). Simultaneous with Harry's death, when "ahead, all he could see, as wide as all the world, great, high, and unbelievably white in the sun, was the square top of Kilimanjaro . . . the hyena stopped whimpering in the night and started to make a strange, human, almost crying sound" (p. 76). As Harry moves progressively into his writing, the "white square top of Kilimanjaro," this process is accompanied by the ignoble presence of vultures. As Harry's death removes him to an unbreachable distance from his ignoble surroundings, the hyena communicates a "strange, human, almost crying sound."

Earl Rovit describes with cold irony the story's ending: "The despicable hyena joins Helen in weeping for the dead artist, because the hyena becomes a distended identification of the audience the artist must serve. Fickle, treacherous, stupid, and cunning at the same time, it is quick to lament the loss of the artist, even as it is quick to harry him when he is alive. Without pushing the metaphor too far, it is fair to say that Hemingway succeeds in insulting his audience beyond endurance, in making the audience eat its own wounds, and liking it."[7] As for the writing retrieved by Harry in the italicized script of the story, opposed in every sense to the aimless, redundant satisfactions of the rich (whose only difference from everyone else is that "they have more money" [p. 72], it records the factual reality of different lives, given once and, unrepeatable, once only.

Readers are quick to recognize the autobiographical—indeed, prophetic—elements of "The Snows of Kilimanjaro." For example, one of Hemingway's biographers, Kenneth Lynn, maintains that "'Kilimanjaro' and 'Macomber' signal a new phase in Hemingway's imaginative life in which the main character dies an untimely death, but not in a way that could be termed suicide. Although this development would eventually include several novel-length works, its most memorable representations were the brief masterpieces produced at its outset. In 'Kilimanjaro' and 'Macomber,' an author who had appeared in *Green Hills of Africa* completely walled up inside a myth of himself was once again in touch with who he actually was" (p. 429). It is not my purpose to dispute Lynn's comparison or his evaluation of *Green Hills of Africa*, except to point out his realist conception of Hemingway's writing during the period in question. Hemingway makes clear that the depicted life that interests biographers like Lynn is "boring." "The Snows of Kilimanjaro," it should be recalled, is a frame story that calls into question, first, the integrative value of self-consciousness as it concerns Harry at the end of his life and the life he adopted among the "rich," and, second, the italicized events of a life that has not been written because he has lived with the "rich," a natural home of self-consciousness and psychological extremes. (Note, as a comparison, the biographical background of his wife's history: a happy marriage with two children, her first husband's death and the experience of dealing with her alienated children, reading and drinking, welcoming successive lovers, the death of one of her children in a plane crash [a decisive event], and, finally,

Harry—"she wanted some one that she respected with her" [p. 61].) Her "nervousness," not to mention Harry's "unpleasantness," is developed in the linear narrative of the story, but another story, the one not written, presents a quite different perspective. The dying writer recalls exactly rendered scenes of Paris that are discontinuous from the narrative. Like the frame story, these, too, are terminal experiences: blankets of snow, a common poverty observed in the Paris years, recollections of war and violent death, gambling, bankruptcies, the suicide of the proprietor of an inn in Triberg, a betrayed love, and a personal memory of a childhood incident where the cabin owned by Harry's grandfather was destroyed by fire, *"and all the guns that had been on deer foot racks above the open fireplace were burned and afterwards their barrels, with the lead melted in the magazines, and the stocks burned away, lay out on the heap of ashes that were used to make lye for the big iron soap kettles, and you asked Grandfather if you could have them to play with and he said, . . . no"* (p. 68). If these vignettes end badly, tragically, if potentialities are exhausted, it is because they stand for a life that has been lived.

We discussed earlier the limitations of realist writing, but a complementary perspective found in Hemingway's new "vignettes" challenges as well "the perspective of the world that we have within everyday experience." Reidar Due, in his examination of Deleuze's philosophy, explains: literary modernity "not only challenges nineteenth-century narrative or realist conventions, it also challenges experience itself. It presents perspectives on life and on ourselves as beings of desire, living in time, using language and interacting physically with the world and these perspectives are not coordinated by pragmatic and ordinary practical concerns or by self-conscious experience."[8] In line with the questioning of ordinary experience is a suspension of the "subject . . . as the center of coordination within experience." In his work on Proust and in the concept of "temporal complexity" found in Proust, Deleuze observes, "the time of a life is not linear and successive, but different lines of development, different aspects of a personality always co-exist."[9]

When Harry dies and the hyena makes a strange sound, it is said that Helen "did not wake. In her dream she was at the house on Long Island and it was the night before her daughter's début. Somehow her father was there and he had been very rude" (p. 77). Her life and

Harry's intersect for "security and comfort," but they are also, individually, different "lines of development." The realist conventions do not capture this and it is of little consequence to Harry, now at the top of Kilimanjaro, where his decomposition will be slow and impersonal.

2

*To Have and Have Not* was published a few months before *The First Forty-Nine Stories*. It was said to incorporate "the mechanics of revolution and what it does to the people in it." As always, it was a matter of Hemingway's relationship to his times. "There are two themes in it," continues his letter to Perkins, "the decline of the individual—The Man Harry—who shows up first in One Trip Across—and his re-emergence as Key West goes down around him—and the story of a shipment of dynamite and all the consequences that happened from it" (*L*, p. 448). Harry, in "The Snows of Kilimanjaro" finds false "security and comfort" with the "rich," not so Harry Morgan, who finds disaster: "a man alone ain't got no bloody f——ing chance." Trying to survive, he has become involved in a bootleg operation; from that beginning, he transports "revolutionaries" to Cuba; sometime later, is observed by a wealthy, administration executive on his rented yacht, dumping illegal contraband. It ends badly. Is this an extension of the "unwritten" experience of "Kilimanjaro"? Is this "ordinary" experience? Not so curiously, the last section of *To Have and Have Not* centers on a writer who, it is safe to say, is a negation of Hemingway's concept of authenticity.

The novel was not meant to be read as a primer on a particular political standpoint, although references to the "New Deal" and its specific programs and policies for helping the Vets in Key West are unsympathetic. Rather, Hemingway focuses on a novelist who uses party affiliation for self-advancement and on "the big things that are happening." We have no argument with Carlos Baker's observation that the novel contains "Hemingway's notes towards the definition of a decaying culture, and his disgust with the smell of death to come."[10] But what of his frame of mind with respect to critics and the reading public during the mid-1930s; what of his sensitivity to the role he seemed to have adopted; what of a novel that explicitly reflects a degree of social and political awareness and a reorientation of his perspective?

# Chapter VI

# "How It Really Was"

*Power in the West is what displays itself the most, and thus what hides itself the most.*

Michel Foucault

*I am no mystic, but to deny it is as ignorant as though you denied the telephone.*

For Whom the Bell Tolls

1

*B*efore beginning to write his novel of the Spanish civil war, Hemingway had been closely involved in the Loyalist cause for three years. As a correspondent for the North American Newspaper Alliance (NANA), he visited Spain for extended periods twice in 1937 and again in 1938. He wrote the script for *The Spanish Earth* and helped finance the production of the film by joining Dos Passos, MacLeish, and Lillian Hellman in founding Contemporary Historians Inc. He addressed the Second American Writer's Congress at Carnegie Hall: "writers have a special stake in fighting fascism because it is the only form of government that will not allow them to tell the truth."[1]

He traveled to Los Angeles seeking financial support of the Loyalist cause. He wrote *The Fifth Column*, a three-act play that made plain his political sympathies. (It was during this period that *To Have and Have Not* was also published, showing a degree of "political" consistency.) Three years of stored experience, in any event, served Hemingway as a catalyst for writing his novel. Not only did he have that experience when he began *For Whom the Bell Tolls*, but he had the formative impressions of his apprentice years and his continuing *afición* for the bullfight and the people of Spain. He had, in short, "the material at hand." Firsthand experience and a writer's intention at a given point in his career unscores his statement that he "decided to write as good and big a novel as I can rather than put off to when older which, the way things go what with war and all, could be an epoch that might never come" (*L*, p. 496).

He would, as always, maintain the customary "idiom," style, and typical preoccupations. There would be no mistaking the author of this novel but it would also be the making of something new that characterized each of Hemingway's works. What, then, had he learned, what had changed, since *Death in the Afternoon* or, for that matter, since *A Farewell to Arms*? What of an evolving career and "political development"—how was his new book an advance on *To Have and Have Not* with its awkward combining of three short stories—a technique he had successfully used in *A Farewell to Arms*? Underlying these questions, it seems clear that *For Whom the Bell Tolls* would be, at the very least, an experimentation. Finally, did the novel succeed; did it meet his expectations and that of his reading public?

Financially, the novel was a tremendous success and its movie rights were quickly sold. As Perkins confided to Fitzgerald, the novel enjoyed the "bourgeois stamp of approval" as a main selection of the Book of the Month Club.[2] In terms of its political reception, "communist reviewers were furious about the book." Writing for the *Daily Worker*, Mike Gold asserted that Hemingway had been "mutilated" by "class egotism." Gold maintained that Hemingway "had joined the Loyalist cause in order to exploit it for personal advantage," an indictment similar to Hemingway's of the corrupt writer in *To Have and Have Not*. Other motives led Dwight Macdonald, in *Partisan Review*, to dismiss the novel; Lionel Trilling, in the same issue of the journal, "felt that the novel had not managed to convey Spain's political tragedy."[3]

The popularity of *For Whom the Bell Tolls* may be explained, in part, by its timeliness, its exoticism, and the fact that it is heroic and romantic, involving, as it does, the story of Robert Jordan, a "dynamiter," and his love for Maria, who faces increasing dangers behind enemy lines. Its hold on readers no doubt stems from its apparent adherence to realist conventions—a three-day, linear development (flashbacks, however, repeatedly interrupt the sequence of events), centering on an extremely self-conscious narrator, a mainstay of traditional fiction. Not incidentally, being a new novel written by Hemingway undoubtedly added to its appeal. The reader could expect a "love interest," uncensored language ("obscenities" included), a modernist bearing, scandals (for example, the betrayal of the communist/Loyalist cause) and the fascination with the "myth" of Hemingway—all abetting the novel's sales. There is no denying the novel's popularity, yet there are two points to be made concerning those elements of the novel that created its appeal. They involve the devices of realist fiction and other modernist elements characteristic of earlier works. But these aspects of the novel are given substantial prominence only to be subverted, in a dramatic modification of his earlier work. The first shift concerns Robert Jordan, a self-conscious narrator. As a narrative grounding, self-consciousness grows increasingly unconvincing, unnatural, and artificial—in short, an exhausted technique. It is not only that the narrator questions himself, it is the artificiality of such expressions as "himself said back to him." The complete passage states: "Listen, he told himself. You better cut this out. This is very bad for you and for your work. Then himself said back to him, You listen, see? . . . I have to keep you straight in your head" (p. 304). There is much more of this disconcerting, internal dialogue, but it is not without a purpose, as we see at the end of the novel: "Once you saw it again as it was to others, once you got rid of your self, the always ridding of self that you had to do in war. Where there could be no self. Where yourself is only to be lost" (p. 447). This "ridding of self" and the rejection of subjectivity opens a space "as it was to others," a new perspective that is essential to Jordan's education, a basic undertaking of the novel, and, possibly, that of the reader's.

The second point concerns the foundational eroticism of "Up in

Michigan" (or the love scenes of *A Farewell to Arms*) as basic to
Hemingway's "naturalness" and as a precursor to the eroticism found
in *For Whom the Bell Tolls*. Similar passages are found in *Green Hills
of Africa*, where an intransitive writing is the hallmark of eroticism
for the writer and a continuation of his "idiom." This modernist
experience finds its elaboration in the Spanish novel. The language
here is precisely one of emotional intensification: "For him it was a
dark passage that led to nowhere, then to nowhere, then again to
nowhere, once again to nowhere, always and forever to nowhere . . .
scaldingly, holdingly all nowhere gone and time absolutely still and
they were both there, time having stopped . . ." (p. 159). Later in the
novel, we find a new conception of time, an altered idiom, and
changed circumstances: "I have never had a wife and now I have thee
for a wife and I am happy" (p. 348) and, followed by "God, he had
done a lot of pretending tonight" (p. 355). The final erotic scene is
like the first but, again, changes can be perceived: "Oh now, now,
now, the only now, and above all now, there is no other now but thou
now and now is thy prophet . . . to earth conclusively now" (p. 379).
The modern understanding of eroticism results from an absent God,
and "transgression" is the new experience of sexuality in a finite
world, but in this last passage, one that was developed through the
mediation of "pretending," Hemingway presents a liturgical form of
the experience. The language has changed and so, too, his relationship
to his earliest, formative impulse. The movement is from a private
(inner) experience to one far more public and, in an odd sense, more
communal. Is this another instance of "as it was to others" that follows the "ridding of self"? Is Hemingway's adoption of ritual form—
the taking of a wife and a religious consecration—a transformation
that suggests the end of Hemingway's modernism, the attenuation of
older beliefs and another stage of development? When Robert Jordan,
late in the novel, admits his ignorance before his involvement with
Pablo's group, is this, perhaps, a recognition that applies to Hemingway? What of his social responsibility as a writer? He had earlier
rejected an alignment with "The Big Things that are Happening" but
is it possible that he found a new political perspective?

  Aside from its relevance to the aesthetic issues of modern novels,
*For Whom the Bell Tolls* sets out an education and development in
which the questions involving Maria and a self-conscious "hero" are

subordinated. An explicit education has Gaylord's for its classroom, the meeting place of the leaders of the communist cause. The other classroom, which is "merely" self-evident, is found in a cave behind the lines among the partisans. The two are opposed in many ways, even though they appear to share similar objectives, the defeat of fascist forces. As seen by Hemingway, the outcome of the struggle between the two positions bears on the possibility of individual freedom, a costly freedom that makes possible a decision, because "no man is an *Iland*, intire of it selfe."

It has been my purpose in discussing Hemingway's works and, especially, those of the 1930s, to show that his perspective was not parochial. Inevitably, his views were shaped by the necessities of writing and career, but the obverse of this statement seems equally valid. *Death in the Afternoon* and *Green Hills of Africa*, as "discursive" experiments, speak to this general understanding and *In Our Time* was not of his time in the late 1930s. Thus, one locates experiments, through "discursive" innovations, to further transformations. Brecht, also acutely sensitive to his times, argued that methods become exhausted and were it not for that eventuality, it would be a sad state for the many who "do not sit at golden tables."[4]

## 2

Robert Jordan is a professor of Spanish at a Montana university who joins the Loyalist cause and who has reason to fear he may lose his post because of his political commitment. This general background is cause for amusement, if not derision, among the partisans and the communist officials at Gaylord's. What then of his new education? As a starting point, it entails a dispossession of self and a new form but not one like "a tragic epic, like the *Iliad*,"[5] as Carlos Baker has said. There is no ultimate return to a homeland in the novel and no "origin" that knits together contradictions. Rather, epic circularity is now a model for a child's amusement, "like a merry-go-round" or, for adults, a wheel of fortune. Each maintains the vestiges of older "recreative" possibilities. Only now they are formal amusements: "a merry-go-round that travels fast, and with a calliope (the Greek muse of eloquence?) for music, and the children ride on cows with gilded horns, and there are rings to catch with sticks, and there is the blue gas-flare-lit early dark of the Avenue du Maine, with fried fish sold from the next stall" or like "a wheel of fortune turning with the leather flaps slapping against the posts of the numbered compartments, and the packages of lump sugar piled in pyramids for prizes" (p. 225). The two wheels, artificially lit, are much alike, with the staccato finality of the "leather flaps slapping" substituted for the "calliope for music" and "gilded horns." Both adults and children are enraptured by the game, the difference lying in an ornamented reality versus the plain fact of numbered compartments. But, with Jordan after his encounter with Pablo, it is another emotional experience: "this is another wheel. This is like a wheel that goes up and down. . . . We are back again now, he thought, and nothing is settled." Although, "the people are waiting, like the men in caps and the women in knitted sweaters, their heads bare in the gaslight and their hair shining, who stand in front of the wheel of fortune as it spins." This last wheel, "up and down," is deadly earnest and Jordan is on it in his conflict with Pablo over dominance and also in his thinking. We, as readers, have our choice of wheels within wheels that radiate inward, that point back to ourselves at different stages of "progress" or disillusionment. "It had been a much simpler world" (p. 228), Jordan acknowledges. In and out of successive wheels, Jordan observes before his death: "I was learning fast there at the end. . . . There's no *one* thing that's true. It's all true" (p. 467).

Robert Jordan is accepted by Karkov and learns to share his political cynicism, a first education; he is accepted by the Spaniards in Pablo's group, the source of a second education. Moreover, in crossing the line from the Russian insiders to the partisans, he enacts a movement in his thinking (and because of his love of Maria) that conditions another education. There are gradations; some thoughts are better than others, one education more grounded than another, with better results. Yet, taken together, they are crucial determinants of the novel's intention. A last set of factors involves Jordan's personal background and his predisposition or "talent" for being educated. He had written a short book on Spain that was the product of ten years of involvement, and he imagines writing a new book based on what he is now learning. Underlying both books, however, is the certain constant: "He liked to know how it really was; not how it was supposed to be" (p. 230). Finally, there is his divided lineage, as the grandson of a man who heroically "fought four years in our Civil War" (p. 336) and in Indian campaigns, and the son of a father who committed suicide: "You have to be awfully occupied with yourself to do a thing like that" (p. 338). According to Golz, who commands the offensive in which Jordan is critically involved, his present circumstances are seen as the product of antithetical impulses. Specifically, Golz characterizes his activity as "very scientific" but questions Jordan about "his bohemianism" behind enemy lines:

> "Look, do you have many girls on the other side of the lines?"
> "No, there is not time for girls."
> "I do not agree. The more irregular the service, the more irregular the life. You have very irregular service. Also you need a haircut." (pp. 7–8)

Background and present circumstances both contribute to Jordan's education, to his receptivity:

> Enemies of the people. That was a phrase he might omit. That was a catch phrase he would skip. That was one thing that sleeping with Maria had done. He had gotten to be as bigoted and hidebound about politics as a hard-shelled Baptist and phrases like enemies of the people came into his mind without his much criticizing them in any way . . . To be bigoted you have to be absolutely sure that you are right and nothing makes that surety and righteousness like continence. Continence is the foe of heresy.
>
> How would that premise hold up if he examined it? That was probably why the Communists were always cracking down on Bohemianism. When you were drunk or when you committed either fornication or adultery you recognized your own personal fallibility of that so mutable substitute for the apostle's creed, the party line. (pp. 163–64)

Jordan's judgment and his critical perceptions have developed. First, he was given a "formal" education at Gaylord's. He had started out a true believer ("it was like being a member of a religious order" [p. 235]) and then he was taught *realpolitik*, a radical complication of his "pure" beliefs (political assassinations, the necessity of lies and rationalizations, the posturing of communist standard-bearers, the internal conflicts for prestige and dominance, and the like). In his second education, he finds the clarification of bohemian excesses outside communist discipline. But here, too, he finds complications: the encounter with Pablo, who threatens Jordan's mission, Pilar's other "bohemianism"—gypsy fortune telling involving Jordan's destiny and culminating in the famous "smell of death" section of the novel—her story of the fascist massacre, and other elements such as Andres's passage through the Loyalist lines or Anselmo's behavior and thoughts or El Sordo's death. In either situation, the world of *realpolitik* or bohemian excesses, "things are not as simple as they seem." Yet, it might be noted, as Deleuze says in his study of another complicated education: "What does violence to us is richer than all the fruits of our goodwill or of our conscious work, and more important than thought is 'what is food for thought.'"[6] Encounters, propitious and involuntary, determine the direction of thought; productive thinking comes *after* an encounter that provokes thought. This might be termed Jordan's first lesson.

To sort out the implicated layers that make up Jordan's learning and, as importantly, how they condition his knowledge and education, it is useful to consider a more fundamental issue concerning what Deleuze calls "the image of thought." This context for thinking is based on presuppositions that were invented at an older time and, then, developed and reinforced over a long history. Because of this, the conditions for thinking in a philosophical context are no longer seen as an "invention" that could have easily been otherwise than they are, but as a *fact* of nature, of our nature. In other words, "the image of thought" stands for what is taken for granted, that seems self-evident, in the activity of thinking, the (unexamined) belief "that thought is the natural exercise of a faculty." Further, this "image" is based on "the presupposition that there is a natural capacity for thought endowed with a talent for truth or an affinity with the true, under the double aspect of a *good will on the part of the thinker* and an *upright nature on the part of thought*."[7] The "image of thought," according to Deleuze, is an essential and unacknowledged thread in the history of philosophy, defining the very conditions for thinking. A further criticism is that thought that accords with volition, from conscious effort, is arbitrary and abstract. It may be logically consistent and produce a variety of truths but it does not confirm a necessary truth. In *Proust & Signs*, Deleuze quotes Proust on the advantages of an artistic work in apprehending truth: "The truths that intelligence grasps directly in the open light of day have something less profound, less *necessary* about them, than those that life has communicated to us *in spite of ourselves* in an impression, a material impression, because it has reached us through our sense, but whose spirit we can extract . . ."[8] The truths that Robert Jordan finds by accident is located in dark places, Pablo's cave and the smoky rooms of Gaylord's, and they result from material impressions in time that forces him to think. "This is because," Deleuze writes, "philosophy, like friendship, is ignorant of the dark regions in which are elaborated the effective forces that act on thought, the determinations that *force* us to think." Goodwill, a condition of philosophy and friendship, discloses the conventional: "Only the conventional is explicit."

To question the assumptions underlying "the image of thought" is to reject the philosophic tradition that sustained it. What, then, did this "image" obscure, what self-evident facts were pushed to the side when this "image" was invented? The immediate answer, it seems obvious, is found in Proust and the artistic creations, including Hemingway's, that value an involuntary and unsought sensation as a stimulus for thought. The antagonism between the poet and philosopher continues. Deleuze of course argues an alternate viewpoint based on his earliest interest in Nietzsche, as does Foucault, who had been closely associated with Deleuze since the 1960s. Foucault, in fact, provides a forceful formulation concerning the aftermath of the "image of thought," as this "image" loses its hold on the philosopher. He also provides another antagonist to the philosopher. In "Truth and Juridical Form," a series of lectures delivered in Brazil in 1973, Foucault developed a provocative thesis, based on his reading of *The Gay Science*, concerning man's "invention" of knowledge. Foucault's summary is direct and unequivocal: "So one can see why Nietzsche declares that it is the philosopher who is the most likely to be wrong about the nature of knowledge, since he always thinks of it in the form of congruence, love, unity, and pacification. Thus, if we seek to ascertain what knowledge is, we must not look to the form of life, of existence, of asceticism that characterizes the philosopher. If we truly wish to know knowledge, to know what it is, to apprehend it at its root, in its manufacture, we must look not to philosophers, but to politicians—we need to understand what the relations of struggle and power are . . . the manner in which things and men hate one another, fight one another, and try to dominate one another, to exercise power relations over one another."[9]

This background helps us understand the limitations of Robert Jordan's first political education with Karkov. Because "it would be interesting for a professor to be educated," Karkov volunteers to be Jordan's mentor. When Jordan informs him that he has read Emil Burns's *Handbook of Marxism*, Karkov approves: "There are fifteen hundred pages and you could spend some time on each page. But there are some other things you should read" (p. 244). Both master and disciple, at this stage, devote themselves to a search and to the boundless opportunities afforded by dialectics. Equally, they share the same preoccupation with the progressive expansion of reason as a totalizing instrument. Reason serves, simultaneously, as an end and as a means for the repeated transformation of unreason, resolving contradictions, and negating negativity. At a practical level, the communist intervention in Spain is an application of dialectics; this explains the Russian emphasis on class oppression and the necessity of discipline among the Spaniards, as the basis for revolution. A product of dialectical thought, discipline finds its justification in a "synthetic" historical resolution. As common goal and common language, reason absolves the necessary injustices of historical development. In short, Jordan's education, following his initial phase as a "true believer," revolves around, at the extreme, a terrorist conception of history and dialectics as terrorist reason. In either case, the present can be sacrificed for the promise of a successful historical resolution.[10] Gaylord's may be the home of a form of theoretical thought that relies on an economic reading of history, but it is also the ground of countless power struggles, passions, hatreds, and, simply stated, the undisguised play of instincts. As presented in the novel, it appears that those who insist on discipline are the least disciplined. (This characterization undoubtedly infuriated Hemingway's communist reviewers.) This perception of the internal politics of communist infighting remains hidden within the intimate confines of Gaylord's. As well, the real background of the "peasant" leaders who were indoctrinated in Russia is maintained as a state secret. In the absence of "pure" beliefs, moral and intellectual concessions are permitted for the "greater cause."

In contrast, Robert Jordan's brief education—in the novel's present tense—arises from a series of heightened experiences that fully "problematize" the nature of dialetics and class warfare at the heart of the Republican cause. In other words, Jordan's new experience calls into question the assumptions of his first education. Where at an earlier time he could accept the communist dogma that the war was essentially a conflict between a powerful ruling class and a generic Spanish "proletariat," he quickly learns that "power is not the property of a class."[11] With General Golz, at the beginning of the novel, he is made to understand the first obstacle in accomplishing what will become an increasingly difficult operation. The objective of "dynamiting" a particular bridge seems a straightforward objective; however, complications are immediately introduced by the issue of timing and the involvement of others in the decisions being made: "They are never my attacks," Golz said. "I make them but they are not mine. The artillery is not mine. I must put in for it . . . Always there is something. Always someone will interfere" (p. 5). Power is a function of a network of relationships, a relation of forces; it is everywhere and nowhere. General Golz realizes that ultimate power is not his and may not exist, but he can act on the actions of others in a variety of ways as others can affect his plans. The action or inaction or untimely action of an artillery barrage conditions the larger action of a general offensive. At the end of the novel we are again shown in great detail the multiplication of power relations when Andres attempts to cross the Loyalist lines. His message to Golz from Jordan, involving the disposition of the enemy forces, is critical to the attack, yet he is made to run an exemplary gauntlet of "power relations." Throughout his passage, he encounters those who assert their superiority or indifference or simple incapacity to help him. Finally, he meets Captain Gomez and Lieutenant-Colonel Miranda and they help him reach his objective but he arrives at Golz's headquarters too late to change the outcome of the offensive. Andres's passage is both an action and an objective but the narrative interest shifts to his unstable relation to others, to the relation of forces at the level of prosaic encounters—from the ground up. Power relations are, at the same time, the most concrete and the most abstract. Foucault further clarifies these examples of Hemingway's formulation of politicized activities: "Obviously, the establishing of power relations does not exclude the use of violence any more than it does the obtaining of consent. . . . The exercise of power can produce as much acceptance as may be wished for: it can pile up the dead and shelter itself behind what threats it can imagine. . . . It is a set of actions on possible actions; it incites, it induces, it seduces, it makes easier or more difficult; it releases or contrives, makes more probable or less; in the extreme, it constrains or forbids absolutely, but it is always a way of acting upon one or more acting subjects by virtue of their acting or being capable of action. A set of actions upon other actions."[12]

Foucault's description of power relations also clarifies other decisive encounters in *For Whom the Bell Tolls*: Jordan's initial meeting with Pablo, the rebellion by Pilar where Pablo is replaced as leader of the partisans, her story of the fascist massacre, the incident, much later in the novel, where Pablo steals blasting caps and escapes in the night. Throughout all of this, we find the unending exercise of power, as "actions upon other actions" with marked effects. As for the extreme form of power relations, "the use of violence," it is the very fabric of Pilar's retelling of the fascist massacre. Pilar's story portrays the extremes of the revolution and the story is presented against the background of economic exploitation, as understood from a Marxist viewpoint, but there is more. Once the *guardia civil* are executed, Pablo's "revolutionary" group takes over a small village and, in a ritualized fashion (reminiscent of the running of the bulls), forces the "capitalists" (landowners, small business proprietors, and political functionaries) to run a deadly gauntlet; once killed, they are thrown from a high cliff to the river below. The dialectic is plain—the overturning of a bourgeois ruling class by a peasant "proletariat"—but the actual procedure and motives are far from clear. Over time, the activity degenerates and "drunkards" (exclusively) man the gauntlet. Yet the seeds of degeneration are present from the beginning. The first to face the gauntlet is the town mayor, Don Benito Garcia, and no one will strike him: "He passed two men, four men, eight men, ten men, and nothing happened." Then, one man does strike the first blow, "That for you, *Cabron*," and the crowd joins him in beating and flailing the mayor. At last, "they dragged him over the walk to the edge of the cliff and threw him over and into the river. And the man who hit him first was kneeling by the edge of the cliff looking over after him and saying, 'The Cabron, The Cabron, Oh, the Cabron!' He was a tenant of Don Benito and they had never gotten along together. There had been a dispute about a piece of land by the river that Don Benito had taken from this man and let to another and this man had long hated him. This man did not join the line again but sat by the cliff looking down where Don Benito had fallen" (pp. 108–109). What then of dialectical reason when the basis of action is a long-held grudge—passion, instinct, and hatred? Pablo is also made understandable in Pilar's version of the massacre. He is intelligent and a good organizer but he is, in addition, a despotic leader with his own agenda. After the massacre, he admits to Pilar that he liked "all of it, except the priest":

> "You didn't like it about the priest?" because I knew he hated priests even worse than he hated fascists.
> "He was a disillusionment to me," Pablo said sadly.

Whether among Gaylord's *intelligencia* or the partisans, passions rule and discipline, including Pablo's organizational ability, is at the service of instincts. Power relations of the most individualizing kind underlie and are expressed in these emotions. As for Jordan's education and the knowledge he gains in his final three days, there is this perspective: "If we truly wish to know knowledge, to know what it is, to apprehend it at its root . . . we need to understand what the relations of struggle and power are . . . the manner in which things and men hate one another, fight one another, and try to dominate one another, to exercise power relations over one another."[13] There are no simple answers, no absolute perspective, Jordan learns: "how little we know of what there is to know" (p. 380). Breaking with the philosophical framework of his first education opens another world of correspondences and new knowledge:

> I wish I were going to live a long time instead of going to die today because I have learned much about life in these four days: more, I think, than in all the other time. I'd like to be an old man and to really know. I wonder if you keep on learning or if there is only a certain amount each man can understand. I thought I knew so many things that I know nothing of. I wish there was more time. (p. 380)

I remarked earlier that Hemingway was suspicious of the radical tendencies of the 1930s. He followed no set party line, a fact evident in *For Whom the Bell Tolls*. The Russian cadre are treated individually in the novel, and those who are the most cynical, who "joke," who question the party line seem the most competent. A character like "Marty" is dogmatic on party matters to the point of madness. In any event, Hemingway's emphasis is on the relation of the individual to the group. Equally, his depiction of Pablo, Pilar, Anselmo, El Sordo, and others is highly individualized as they relate to the group. In fact, he observes that what characterizes a Spaniard is his extreme identification with those aspects of his life that come closest to best defining him: "A Spaniard was only really loyal to his village in the end. First Spain, of course, then his own tribe, then his own province, then his village, his family and finally his trade. If you knew Spanish he was prejudiced in your favor, if you knew his province it was that much better, but if you knew his village and his trade you were in as far as any foreigner ever could be." Expressing individuality in an almost emblematic fashion, Spaniards in the novel relate to a group and relate most to an individualizing group, "a trade." "Of course they turned on you. They turned on you often but they always turned on every one. They turned on themselves, too. If you had three together, two would unite against one, and then the two would start to betray each other. Not always, but often enough for you to take enough cases and start to draw it as a conclusion." Jordan, who is accepted by the Spaniards, "as far as any foreigner ever could," notes the reality of human nature as a stubborn assertion of will, whimsicality, and impracticality and continually interrupts his thoughts to remind himself of the urgency of his mission: "This is no way to think; but who censored his thinking? Nobody but himself" (pp. 135–36). The concern in Jordan's "musings" always returns to the necessity of an action. The product of his questioning of presuppositions is not relativism or passivity that cripples the ability to act. Rather, his thinking opens possibilities for thought and action, since the exercise of power shows "a mode of action upon the actions of others" or "the government of men by other men." Importantly, as it relates to Hemingway's novel, "power is exercised only over free subjects, and only insofar as they are 'free.' By this we mean individual or collective subjects who are faced with a field of possibilities in which kinds of conduct, several ways of reacting and modes of behavior are available. Where the determining factors are exhaustive, there is no relationship of power; slavery is not a power relationship . . ."[14]

Robert Jordan lies on the pine needles waiting for the approaching cavalry. He is badly wounded and he has sent Maria away with the others. He has many thoughts, he continues to worry, and his pain is becoming unbearable. He thinks of killing himself. And then feels fortunate. "That is the best. And who says it is not true? Not you. You don't say it, any more than you would say the things did not happen that happened. Stay with what you believe now. Don't get cynical. The time is too short and you have just sent her away. Each one does what he can" (p. 466). A limited action is given as a part of the whole and, as presented at the end of *Death in the Afternoon*: "Let those who want to save the world if you can get to see it clear and as a whole. Then any part you make will represent the whole if it's truly made" (p. 278).

## 3

Of course, Hemingway was not without a model, other books and influences, in his decision "to write as good and big a novel as I can" (*L*, p. 496). From any number of documents that date from the mid-1930s, it seems reasonable to assume that a particularly important model was Dostoyevsky. Fitzgerald, who was surely aware of Hemingway's priorities and who continued to support his career, said that *To Have and Have Not* had passages that were "right up with Dostoievski [*sic*] in their undeflected intensity."[15] In *Green Hills of Africa*, Dostoyevsky is the last author mentioned in the short list of dominant modern writers who "are forged in injustice as a sword is forged"; and, in the same period, Hemingway included *The Brothers Karamazov* and "any other two" novels by Dostoyevsky in brief lists of decisive modern works.[16] "Like having a great treasure given to you" is Hemingway's description of his discovery of Russian writers in *A Moveable Feast*, where he says of Dostoyevsky: "there were things believable and not to be believed, but some so true they changed you as you read them; frailty and madness, wickedness and saintliness, and the insanity of gambling were there to know as you knew the landscape and the roads in Turgenev and the men and the fighting in Tolstoi" (p. 132). In general terms, modern Russian authors—Turgenev, Tolstoi, and Dostoyevsky—established a literary itinerary for Hemingway's most successful novels, *The Sun Also Rises*, *A Farewell to Arms*, and *For Whom the Bell Tolls*. Moreover, his deep interest in these writers established his difference and the individualized development that, in turn, distanced him from his Paris influences. When he told Pound of his discovery, he was advised, "keep to the French" (p. 133). His friend, Evan Shipman, said, "don't let it tempt you, Hem" (p. 136), when Hemingway remarked: "How can a man write so badly, so unbelievably badly, and make you feel so deeply?" (p. 135). In terms of Pound's credo of the *mot juste* and the dominant influence of French writers upon expatriate writers in the 1920s, Russian writers stood for temptation, heresy, and the abdication of modernist beliefs. Again, in a letter to Faulkner, Hemingway states the central importance of the Russian influence: "You should always write your best against dead writers that we know what stature (not stature: evocative power) that they have and best them one by one. Why do you want to fight Dostoyevsky in your first fight? Beat Turgenieff.... Then nail yourself DeMaupassant [*sics*]. ... Then try and take Stendhal. (Take him and we're all happy.)" Turning to contemporaries and the importance of Flaubert as an author responsible for the essential direction of modern writing, he addresses the issue of a writer's development:

> But don't fight with the poor pathological characters of our time (we won't name). You and I can both beat Flaubert who is our most respected, honored master. But to do that you have to be able to accept the command of a battalion when it is given (when you are a great company commander) to relinquish it to be second in command of a regiment (walk with shits nor lose the common touch) and then be able to take a regiment when you loathe the takeing [*sic*] of it and were happy where you were (or were unhappy but didn't want to go over Niagara Falls in a barrel) (I can't go higher in this hierarchy because I have no higher experience and anyway probably bore the shit out of you). (pp. 624–25)

The military metaphor suggests a breaking out of provincial and limited preoccupations, the assumption of responsibility on a larger front and the necessity of more risk in the process. If Dostoyevsky had moved him so strongly, in spite of their marked differences, Hemingway's challenge in *For Whom the Bell Tolls* had been to achieve the same impact, the same evocative power and intensity.

In addition, it may have seemed appropriate to deal with the Russian involvement in Spain by using a Russian "instrument." Works such as *Notes from the Underground, Crime and Punishment, The Idiot,* and *The Brothers Karamazov* contested the apparent "progress" of reason and may have suggested to Hemingway a way to capture the excessive nature of Spanish individuality in a world where there were "things believable and not to be believed." Both writers were attracted to the exceptional nature of prosaic reality. In a letter to Strakhov, Dostoyevsky defined his "idea of reality in art":

> what most people will call almost fantastic and an exception some-times constitutes for me the very essence of reality. The ordinariness of events and the conventional view of them is not realism in my opinion but, indeed, the very opposite of it. In every newspaper you find accounts of the most real facts which are also the most strange and most complex. To our writers they appear fantastic and they do not even bother about them, and yet they are reality because they are facts. Who is there to notice, explain, and describe them? They happen every minute and every day and they are not an *exception*.[17]

Attuned to their present reality, both writers focus on "facts," as found in common reality, "the very essence of reality." And for both writers, as related to the nihilism or decadence of their time, the focus is on the fate of the individual when faced with the reality of the "Glass Palace."

In a letter to Dos Passos, cited earlier, he says: "I don't believe and can't believe in too much government—no matter what good is the end. To hell with the Church when it becomes a State and the hell with the State when it becomes a church" (*L*, p. 419). In another letter from the same period: "You write like a patriot and that is your blind spot. I've seen a lot of patriots and they all died just like anybody else if it hurt bad enough and once they were dead their patriotism was only good for legends; it was bad for their prose and made them write bad poetry. If you are going to be a great patriot i.e. loyal to any existing order of government (not one who wishes to destroy the existing for something better) you want to be killed early if your life and works won't stink" (*L*, p. 432). From Hemingway's perspective, the possibility of an ongoing career requires that the writer stand to the side of events, to adopt a stance of apparent marginality. He also understands that "the ordinariness of events and the conventional view of them" is not a true picture. Things are not what they seem.

In an essay entitled "Secular Criticism," Edward Said generously defines the activity of the critic. It is a position that easily accommodates Hemingway's stance in *For Whom the Bell Tolls*, in suggesting that the purpose of criticism is precisely one of social, political, and cultural resonance. Always in the best sense, it is a matter of *for whom the bell tolls*. Said begins by asserting the need for a positioning: "the individual consciousness placed at a sensitive nodal point" and further explains:

> On the one hand, the individual mind registers and is very much aware of the collective whole, context, or situation in which it finds itself. On the other hand, it is precisely because of this awareness—a worldly self-situating, a sensitive response to the dominant culture—that the individual consciousness is not naturally and easily a mere child of the culture, but a historical and social actor in it. And because of that perspective, which introduces circumstance and distinction where there had only been conformity and belonging, there is distance, or what we might call criticism. A knowledge of history, a recognition of social circumstance, an analytic capacity for making distinctions: these trouble the quasi-religious authority of being comfortably at home among one's own people, supported by known powers and accepted values, protected against the outside world.[18]

As they relate to *For Whom the Bell Tolls*, two points bear emphasis in Said's concept of "secular criticism." The first concerns the rejection of "natural" filiations, as Said writes, "the quasi-religious authority of being comfortably at home," for the riskier activity of forming affiliations that cut across the stubborn demarcations of race, nation, language, and so forth. High modernism, in Said's view, is populated by countless figures (childless couples, orphaned, etc.) who manifest "the difficulties of filiation." "But no less important," he adds, "is the second part of the pattern, which is immediately consequent upon the first: the pressure to produce new and different ways

of conceiving human relationships."[19] As Hemingway's understanding of new relationships shows in his handling of the partisan
group, social arrangements replacing family structure are precarious.
A good example of this shift is Anselmo, who is a reliable guide to
Robert Jordan but who has lost the guiding influence of church and
family. The second point arising from Said's discussion concerns a
system of exclusion where what is not part of "us" is relegated to a
nonexistence. Extending this observation, Said asserts that secular
criticism opposes the certainty of critical methods that become *the
method*, "blithely determining what they discuss, heedlessly con-
verting everything into evidence for the efficacy of the method, care-
lessly ignoring the circumstances out of which all theory, system, and
method ultimately derive."

·The importance of circumstances for Hemingway, the conditions
"out of which" his work was shaped, determines the "difference of us
guys." His background, as he explains in his letter to Faulkner, was
not only one in which he had severed his filial ties but fully that of a
"displaced person":

> Difference with us guys is I always lived out of country (as merce-
> nary or patriot) since kid. My own country gone. Trees cut down.
> Nothing left but gas stations, sub-divisions where we hunted snipe
> on the prairie, etc. Found good country outside, learned language as
> well as I know English, and lost it the same way. Most people don't
> know this. Dos always came to us as a tourist. I was always makeing
> a liveing [*sics*], paying my debts and always stayed to fight. Been
> chickenshit displaced person since can remember but fought each
> time before we lost . . .

The passage describes Hemingway's situation, as it does Robert
Jordan's. He, too, is a displaced person who has stayed to fight. He is
trusted because of his facility with Spanish and Pilar, who is the writer
Jordan wishes to be—"God, how she could tell a story. She's better
than Quevedo, he thought. He never wrote the death of any Don
Faustino as well as she told it. I wish I could write well enough to
write that story, he thought" (p. 134)—provides yet another implicit
education. Pilar is the critical, secular consciousness of the novel; she
is the book's intelligence. Her circumstances are made plain since they
underlie her acute discriminations; she observes differences in and

between individuals, events, and the history she has experienced. She stands as Hemingway's principle of creative activity, a female principle that engenders the best story in the novel. She guides the unfolding of *For Whom the Bell Tolls*. In this, one finds another departure from Hemingway's earlier work, a destiny of life as lived.

## 4

The 1930s was a period of accomplishment for Hemingway. Over the span of twenty years he had published three collections of short stories, a satire, a roman à clef (*The Sun Also Rises*), a semi-historical novel (*A Farewell to Arms*), a book of natural history, a safari book, a proletariat novel, and a play. As Michael Reynolds says, "*For Whom the Bell Tolls* was his epic novel just as 'The Snows of Kilimanjaro' was his epic short story. . . . The critics who said that he was repeating himself were missing the obvious. Always experimenting, always reaching beyond his last effort, Hemingway never repeated the form."[20] Another constant was Hemingway's obsession and self-absorption, as they involved his writing, his works, his career, in which it was always a matter of knowing what there is to know. A basic criterion underlies his efforts: "a writer should be of as great probity and honesty as a priest of God. He is either honest or not . . . after one piece of dishonest writing . . . which he knows in his inner self is not true, for no matter what patriotic motives, then he is finished. . . . And he will never be at peace with himself because he has deserted his one complete obligation" (p. 55). Some of his works were well received, others not. With *To Have and Have Not*, he wrote a novel that pits an individual against the system, but failed to provide a convincing resolution. The last section of the novel and the events that lead to Harry Morgan's defeat seem arbitrary at best. And yet it was received by many as a political success and an indication that Hemingway's viewpoint had matured. With *For Whom the Bell Tolls*, whose critical reception was less than positive in political quarters, the action is integral and coherent. Clearly, methods become exhausted and it is necessary to change. It is in this sense that Hemingway subordinated his modernist beliefs to a new perception of political reality *from the ground up*, as a grass-roots point of view. In the "ridding of self" that allows the reality of power relations to emerge is a recognition of the freedom that is essential to the exercise of power—that is, the new basis for political action. The individual, as Harry Morgan would have it, is not powerless. And the change that the Spanish novel looks for is the result of numerous individual actions by guerrilla forces behind enemy lines. A common—or is it uncommon?—reality awaits a free agent, as it does El Sordo:

> Dying was nothing and he had no picture of it nor fear of it in his mind. But living was a field of grain blowing in the wind on the side of a hill. Living was a hawk in the sky.
>
> Living was an earthen jar of water in the dust of the threshing with the grain flailed out and the chaff blowing. Living was a horse between your legs and a carbine under one leg and a hill and a valley and a stream with trees along it and the far side of the valley and the hills beyond. (pp. 312–13)

And moments before his death, we observe Robert Jordan: "He was completely integrated now and he took a good long look at everything. Then he looked up at the sky. There were big white clouds in it. He touched the palm of his hand against the pine needle where he lay and he touched the bark of the pine trunk that he lay behind" (p. 471). He is integrated and he will make a difference: "*And if you wait and hold them up even a little while or just get the officer that may make a difference. One thing well done can make - - - - - - -*" (p. 470). Yes, make a difference, always the difference of the achieved work that breaks preestablished patterns, always more difference, in a world moving heedlessly, blithely, toward similarity.

*Conclusion*

# "Myself I Must Remake"

> *Grant me an old man's frenzy,*
> *Myself I must remake*
> *Till I am Timon or Lear*
> *Or that William Blake*
> *Who beat upon the wall*
> *Till truth obeyed his call.*
>
> Yeats

*What awaits this ultimate man, capable once more and for the last time of not stopping at the sufficiency which he has reached, is a limit-experience. It is the desire of man without desire, the dissatisfaction of those who are satisfied "in all things."* . . .

Blanchot, L'entretien infini

*"Well, Papa," I said, "like Mr. James Durante says, 'It's the conditions that prevail.'"*

*"Conditions are what you make them, boy. Now here's what we do."*

Hotchner, Papa Hemingway

1

*F*ollowing WWII, Hemingway began writing a series of inter-related stories that he referred to as "The Land, Sea, and Air Book." Of the four separate volumes eventually created out of this work, only two saw publication while he was alive: *Across the River and Into the Trees* and *The Old Man and the Sea*, published, respectively, in 1950 and 1952. The first novel received extremely negative reviews and, to this day, has been largely ignored, while the reception of *The Old Man and the Sea* has been far different, earning Hemingway (finally) the Nobel Prize. Concerning the larger project he had originally planned and that he continued to rework in his last years, they have been described by Rose Marie Burwell in her study of the posthumous novels in this fashion: "In their totality, the four narratives record Hemingway's fifteen-year search for a form and a style that would express his reflexive vision of the artist."[1] Burwell argues that these works showed a discernable movement toward "post-modern narratives" in the creation of protean characters "unknown in English literature" before his time. But this focus carries much further back to his "protean" beginning. Whether *A Moveable Feast* is a memoir or a fiction is of little consequence as it describes his obsession with writing and how his obsession involved a writing that turned back on itself, a self-reflexiveness that contains the "inner experience." When looked at from the perspective of Hemingway's career, the last two books he published are far more revealing about Hemingway's intentions, especially if we consider how a career at a given moment in time circumstances the work that is produced. We saw earlier Hemingway's examination of the relationship of career and work in *Green Hills of Africa* and how both internal and external factors condition the continued elaboration of his text. Internally, the concern is one of repetition and innovation, while external constraints of dissemination, publication, and public reception also affect the production of a work. In the case of *Across the River and Into the Trees* and *The Old Man and the Sea*, Hemingway's career or, better yet, his perception of his career is one in which he sees himself as nearing the end. What is it we find at this stage? Possibilities have become far more restrictive and among the few remaining ones, "recapitulations are common"—thus, the process found in *A Moveable Feast*. But so, too, one finds "antidotes to the end of a career." Yeats's frenzy and a desired transfiguration is a well-known antidote to old age and the end of a career. As Said explains in *Beginnings*, "a recapitulary, essential image" or the invasion of the text by "explanation"[2] are others. Or, perhaps, there is a mixing of all these elements or a single powerful medication that keeps Richard Cantwell alive to finish his story or there is raw fish that Santiago eats to keep up his strength while fighting his "unending" marlin.

Burwell's reading of Hemingway's posthumous works focuses on his androgynous preoccupation with creativity. Unfortunately, she suggests that supporting this "theory" as its justification is the fact that his mother dressed him like a girl when he was young, a biographical linking of the life and the work in ways that are not especially illuminating. It might be better to realize that a life and a work are not the same in all respects and that they might well be at cross-purposes. "What organizes a literary career," Said writes, "is the constantly tantalizing dilemma of whether the writing life conflicts with, runs parallel to, uniquely imitates, or finally stunts empirical existence." Even more to the point, "a literary career does not reflect the man's life, it absorbs it, overwhelms it, gets on top of it, in Norman O. Brown's phrase."[3] Finally, with specific regard to the androgynous theme in Hemingway's last works, a broader view might also be salutary: "As an alternative, a literary career begins—as we saw above—by being different from all other sorts of life. Yet such difference is haunted by a certain sameness, so powerful is the image of physical engenderment, and so common both to writing and procreation the notion that what one makes is one's child, one's progeny, one's temporal legacy. . . . A central symbol for the modern producing writer depicts the physical transfer of an image from man's sexual-procreative life to his artistic one. A writer's writing, in other words, is the result of daring to apply sexual energy or attention to the act of writing."[4] In making this point, Said draws on a wide and heterogeneous set of examples: Flaubert, Joyce, Mallarmé, Yeats, Conrad, Wilde, Proust, and Lawrence. The list is far from exhaustive but it has the merit of showing that Hemingway's "strangeness" from an artistic standpoint is commonplace. As guidelines, Said's observations provide a useful context from which to examine Hemingway's last two reflexive experiments.

2

*Across the River and Into the Trees* condenses the work of a lifetime, as does, more acutely, *The Old Man and the Sea*. Both books are lessons learned and their protagonists have completed their education. Both are now in a position to tutor the young, whether it is T5 Jackson and Renata or Santiago's disciple, Manolin. The education of *For Whom the Bell Tolls* is now reversed, but in distinctive fashions, in keeping with quite different teachers. The protagonists in both novels are "strange," where one speaks from bitterness and the other out of serenity. In either case, they faithfully reflect the vocations or "trade" of a lifetime. Their relationship to their life's work is also unconventional; having learned the requirements of their "trade," they nevertheless resist the lure of normative behavior—what they should have done and how they should behave now. Colonel Cantwell, broken in rank from brigadier general, has an abiding suspicion of those who "went by the book" (p. 38), while Santiago, as perceived by other fishermen in his village, "was now definitely and finally *salao*, which is the worst form of unlucky" (p. 9). Yet both have had impressive backgrounds and both now face the ravages of old age and, in the case of Cantwell, imminent death. The knowledge they have accumulated and its reflection on Hemingway's craft is presented in a cryptic, even prosaic, form. For Santiago, such things as laying out his fishing lines to better his chances at finding fish, baiting his hooks, and rowing "gently to keep the lines straight up and down and at their proper depths" (p. 32), reading the skies for the possibility of storms, and, more generally, the "tricks" he learned over a lifetime of marlin fishing—all these things sustain him while fishing and they are also his legacy to a young boy who will become his posterity. With Cantwell, two students attend his lessons: T5 Jackson and Renata. The former is a poor, dismissive student, "one of those sad Americans" (p. 61), while the latter falls in love with her instructor. Similar to Santiago's, the lessons imparted by Colonel Cantwell are close to home, relate to his personal experience, and concern, as an example, the ability to withstand an Austrian offensive during WWI, "to break through at the angle where the Sile River and the old bed of the Piave were the only lines of defense" (p. 37). All these elements (and there are many more) are given as integral elements of either novel, but they inevitably point back to Hemingway's recognition that he was coming to the end of his career. There is also the general prescription found at any moment in Hemingway's career: "he liked to think about all things he was involved in" (p. 105). Both "recapitulary" narratives bear closer attention.

## 3

Cantwell's story begins with a physical examination, followed by a journey with Jackson from Trieste to Venice, through country that Cantwell had fought in as a young man. A variety of subjects are discussed with Jackson, including Jackson's rudimentary theory of art: "all they got in the local museum is arrow heads, war bonnets, different scalps . . . photographs of Liver Eating Johnson" (pp. 24–25). Cantwell had been discussing Renaissance Italian painters and architects (or rather Cantwell has been lecturing on the subject) and Jackson, that "sad American" type, shows himself a poor audience. Cantwell provides an interesting history of Venice, its evolution from the ruins of Torcello as a defensive position against invading Visigoths, and then condescendingly:

> "Am I boring you Jackson?"
> "No sir. I had no idea who pioneered Venice." (p. 35)

Cantwell provides background on the construction of St. Mark's and Jackson replies: "St. Mark's square is where the pigeons are and where they have that big cathedral that looks sort of like a moving picture palace, isn't it" (p. 36). Cantwell gives it another try: "There's plenty more I could show you, but I think we probably ought to roll now. But take one good look at it. This is where you can see how it all happened. But nobody ever looks at it from here." Jackson replies: "It's a beautiful view. Thank you, sir." Representing Hemingway at a critical point in his career, Cantwell's truculence and high-handedness stems in part from the nature of his audience, and the distance between the two in artistic taste and in background could not be greater. Had Hemingway's audience changed or was it the problems he had always had with the misunderstanding, condemnation, or appreciation for the wrong reasons, of his critics? In this respect, Cantwell observes that he had discovered the best vantage point, "this is where you can see how it all happened." Tellingly, "nobody ever looks at it from here." Hemingway, who had spent a lifetime pursuing his particular literary objective, together with his readers and critics fail to share a common viewpoint. Readers have no interest in seeing "how it all happened." As Renata observes later in the novel: "Every day is a disillusion," to which Cantwell replies:

> "No. Every day is a new and fine illusion. But you can cut out everything phony about the illusion as though you would cut it with a straight-edge razor." (p. 213)

There is the emphatic comparison in the novel of those who have directly experienced battle and the "political" generals who were never at the front. At the extreme of this opposition are the hated Milanese war profiteers. Renata's "illusions" are clarity itself when considered in the light of Hemingway's conception of the elements that govern his works. With regard to "The Order," a fanciful secret society made up of five members, it serves as a fiction within a fiction, named "in honor" of *Cabarellos de Brusadelli*, a notorious war profiteer. "The Order" is a parody, denouncing an empty form. The same attitude applies to the revealing of the "Supreme Secret" of "The Order" during Renata's initiation: "Love is love and fun is fun. But it is always so quiet when the gold fish die" (p. 248). Empty toast, empty secret, empty "Order," empty "those behind the rear lines"— all "illusions" with "everything phony" cut out.

Parody, not to mention self-parody, is constant throughout the novel. The career, the "trade," has transformed Hemingway into a thing of the book. Underlying this unmistakable reality are the tensions that arise from his perception of his career at the end point and this tension played out in Cantwell's struggle with himself. Arguing with the *Gran Maestro* at the Hotel Gritti, Cantwell thinks to himself: "The hell with you, he said to himself. Cut it out and be a human being when you're half a hundred years old" (p. 65). There are many other scenes where he reminds himself not to be brutal, a "tough guy." His understandable concern with "empirical existence," the fact that he knows he is dying, is the source of the tension between a career, Cantwell's "trade," and being a "human being." There are other indications of the last stages of career in the novel in the explicit literary references to King Lear and to Shakespeare—"He writes like a soldier himself" (p. 159)—and to a slightly adumbrated William Blake—"Why have I never seen a gondola before? What hand or eye framed that dark-ed symmetry?" (p. 140)—or the lament of "*Où sont les neiges d'autan?*" (p. 107).

Cantwell has become bored with his "trade":

"Does this bore you? It bores the hell out of me . . ."

"Nobody shares this trade with anybody," the Colonel told her. "I'm just telling how it works. I can insert anecdotes to make it interesting, or plausible." (p. 126)

"Who wants true combat? But here it is, Daughter, on the telephone and later I will put in the sounds and smells and anecdote about who was killed when and where if you want them." (p. 225)

These are, indeed, "recapitulary" notations. (Recall Hemingway's earliest reference to anecdotes after writing *The Sun Also Rises*.) But it is more than that as Cantwell presents a dispassionate dissection of Hemingway's technique, a condensation of a working method at a great remove—as on the telephone.

Other signs of self-reflexiveness are found throughout the novel. Colonel Cantwell and Renata converse in Spanish: "'It isn't much of a trade is it?' He said *oficio* instead of trade, because they spoke Spanish together too, when they left French, and when they did not wish to speak English before other people. Spanish is a rough language, the Colonel thought, rougher than a corncob sometimes. But you can say what you mean in it and make it stick" (pp. 89–90). The novel functions as a handbook for Hemingway's writing and, importantly, in this last passage, it sets out a strange ideal for his language ("rougher than a corncob"), which is foreign to English-speaking readers—the message seems clear, he does not communicate with his reader even when he uses language in which "you can say what you mean in it." Later on, there is a synoptic discussion of writing that reinforces this view of language. 'You ought to write,' the girl said. 'I mean it truly. So someone would know about such things.' Colonel Cantwell disagrees:

> "I have not the talent for it and I know too much. Almost any liar writes more convincingly than a man who was there." (p. 128)

The explanation that follows re-creates some of the reflections found in *Green Hills of Africa*, with an emphasis placed on those generals who write memoirs, "sensitive" boys who write out of their "valid first impressions," those who write for profit, and, then, exceptions to this standard such as Maurice de Saxe, Frederick the Great, and T'sun Su. As for Colonel Cantwell: "But I don't write, Daughter" (p. 129). Rather, at this stage of his career, he achieves a perspective that is beyond fiction, unlike the dutiful memoirs he has read: "Making things clear is my main trade" (p. 138). *Across the River and Into the Trees* is a book of explanation, a book of judgment based on lessons learned: "I don't hate anything, Daughter . . . I only have a point of view, arrived at after careful consideration, and an estimate of their capabilities" (p. 213).

Cantwell does relent and tells his story at the end of the novel, the "true" story of his experience in WWII. But again the diffidence is unmistakable: "So we fought. It is dull but it is informative. This is the way it goes if anyone is ever interested, which I doubt" (p. 221). In spite of the note of disillusionment, the story (writing)—an offensive Colonel Cantwell commanded in the Hurtgen Forest from the front lines and the fatal mistake of Allied aviation bombing his infantry—recalls the best passages of his earlier novels (i.e., the description of the retreat in *A Farewell to Arms*). This story that results from Renata's urging is framed by Cantwell and Renata's "illicit relationship."

As another aspect of a late career development, this May–December love is a fantasy, specifically a fantasy of engenderment. Much like the relationship of Robert Jordan and Maria, the fantasy bears no legitimate offspring.

> "We owe nothing," the Colonel said.
> "Not a thing."
> "Will you marry me and will we have five sons?"
> "I will! I will."
> "The thing is that, would you?"
> "Of course." . . .
> They stood there and kissed each other true.
> "I have a disappointment for you, Richard." (p. 105)

As a substitution for the "disappointment," Renata presents Cantwell with her portrait, whose provenance is of special interest in Hemingway's retrospective on his career, not to mention his other posthumous novels. Again Said's discussion of the literary career is pertinent in outlining the coincidence of career and the "image of physical engenderment, where what a writer makes with his writing is one's child, one's progeny, one's temporal legacy" (p. 263). However, in place of a physical issue, the artist engenders an illicit image, illicit in that it takes from his life the sexual energy that bears children and redirects it to the creation of an image. The Renata/Cantwell love is barren, fated to be without issue from the beginning, while the portrait that she gives to Cantwell is a classic composition:

> It was a beautiful portrait, neither cold, nor snobbish, nor stylized, nor modern. It was the way you would want your girl painted if Tintoretto were still around and, if he were not around, you settled for Velasquez.
>
> It was not the way either of them painted. It was simply a splendid portrait painted, as they sometimes are, in our time. (p. 137)

(Did Hemingway intend for us to think, reflexively, of *In Our Time?*) The painter of this classic portrait is also of interest: "He is a very good painter, but he has false teeth in front because he was a little bit *pédéraste* once and other *pédérasts* attacked him one night on the Lido when there was a full moon" (p. 92). The long debate over pederasty in Greek culture need not concern us. More to the point is an issueless sexual relationship as the basis for the transference of sexual energy to an illicit image, as done by "a very good painter" and as a reflection of Hemingway looking back on his career and the reduction of his empirical life to the demands of a literary career.

We have come full circle, except for the duck hunting in the Venetian marshes, which begins and ends the novel and which frames the novel (the novel as frame within frame). Here, we find a recalcitrant guide because he has misidentified Cantwell (who is out of uniform) and a disappointing hunt because of an unexpected weather front that freezes the lagoon. These conditions greet Cantwell's last action. At the end of the novel, T5 Jackson waits to drive the colonel back to Trieste. In the backseat of his Buick, Cantwell recalls General Thomas J. Jackson's last words: "'Order A.P. Hill to prepare for action.' Then some more delirious crap. Then he said, 'No, no, let us cross the river and rest under the shade of the trees.'" Cantwell suffers his last heart attack in the Buick, having left a note for Jackson with instructions to return the portrait of Renata (and her expensive earrings) to the Hotel Gritti in the event of his death. Jackson's surly reaction is a final insult: "'They'll return them all right, through channels' . . . and put the car in gear" (p. 283). In his last novel Hemingway produced an examination of his career and of his current situation at the time the novel was written. Perhaps it was a last "will and testament." It presents, in digest form, the "tricks of the trade," the perception of "political generals," politics generally, and the excessive corruption of war profiteers. It shows the enthusiasm of youth, when Cantwell fought on the Italian front and, always, the effects of chance events. It contains all of Hemingway's preoccupations as a writer, beginning with his perception of his audience, both good and bad. The lowering of the taste and education of the reading public concerned him as early as *The Sun Also Rises* and found its explicit assessment in *Death in the Afternoon*: "A bullfighter will not be better than his audience very long. If they prefer tricks to sincerity they soon get the tricks" (p. 163). Audience misconceptions have, in part, led to what he has been made of in his life as a modern writer, and the novel plays out this inflated image. The reflection on craft as "rough as corncob" and familiar as a foreign (Spanish) tongue also indicates new and extreme formulations. More revealing still is the acknowledgment of the illicit transference of the act of physical engenderment to the literary creation that is made explicit in the novel. That T5 Jackson decides to have Cantwell's "possessions" returned "through channels" is an ironic reversal of an action and judgment, now the business of his superiors in Trieste, one that had, not so long ago, reduced him in rank from brigadier general to full colonel. What of Hemingway's audience and his feelings toward his readers?

4

Youthful strength, care-free exuberance, and the resiliency found in certain places—this makes up the substance of Santiago's dreams:

> He dreamed of Africa when he was a boy and the long golden beaches and the white beaches, so white they hurt your eyes, and the high capes and the great brown mountains. . . . He only dreamed of places now and of the lions on the beach. They played like young cats in the dusk . . . (pp. 24–25)

Wide awake, being pulled farther out into the Gulf Stream by the marlin, Santiago gathers his strength and he remembers, "the time in the tavern at Casablanca when he played the hand game with the great negro from Cienfuegos . . . for a long time after that everyone had called him 'The Champion' (pp. 69–70). Colonel Cantwell has had similar dreams, perhaps not as evocative, yet faithful to his nature and trade: "Not bad dreams. But usually strange ones. Combat dreams, always, for a while after combat. But then strange dreams about places mostly. We live by accident of terrain, you know. And terrain is what remains in the dreaming part of your mind" (p. 117). Old age and youthfulness—perhaps the desire for youth in old age— predominate in Hemingway's last works. The less obvious and more permanent dream material concerns places and terrain: "we live by accident of terrain." The same might be said by Santiago of the Gulf Stream. What might this mean? Whether in the Gulf Stream, the site of a "monumental" struggle, or on a battlefield, "terrain" defines natural conditions, propitious or not, which determine the outcome of an engagement. (Cantwell supplies numerous examples, while, for Santiago, the reality of his world involves depths, distances, sea conditions, another natural environment.) If dreams are indeed the mechanism for wish fulfillment, Cantwell/Santiago (née Hemingway) seek perpetual youth and ideal conditions for the work to be done. This is a dream at the end of a career.

A dream is a dream, but with Hemingway it is made into a literal dream narrative with the ideal conditions of Venice, the "Sea City," and "*la mar.*" (The concern with place also underscores the metaphorical settings of Hemingway's unpublished novels, contemporary with the writing of *The Old Man and the Sea*.) The dream narrative is carried through to the end, but there are obstacles. Nevertheless, its function is to leave the past behind: "The thousand times that he had proved it meant nothing. Now he was proving it again. Each time was a new time and he never thought about the past when he was doing it" (p. 66). There is no loneliness while working. Santiago has company at sea—birds, dolphin, flying fish, then a special invited guest, the incredible marlin; he has conversations and talks to himself. Cantwell, too, remarks: "I'm not lonely when I'm working. I have to think too hard to ever be lonely" (p. 99). Santiago, for his part, has gone out too far and his luck is changed, as he is fully consumed by his battle with the marlin. The fish is carefully hooked, its weight estimated, adjustments made throughout the struggle. It carries Santiago further out into the Gulf Stream for two full days. Santiago is pulled by the fish and feels the pain in his hands and back. He is diligent throughout, careful not to break his hold on the marlin. Finally, the marlin begins circling his skiff. The end is near and Santiago is "proving it again." This condensed, bloodless outline suggests Hemingway's writing method; it "explains" how, unexpectedly, a short story expands into a novel, out of the "hidden depths." It is arguably his difference or his perception of his difference from writers like Gertrude Stein as seen in *A Moveable Feast*: "Writing every day made her happy, but as I got to know her better I found that for her to keep happy it was necessary that this steady daily output, which varied with her energy, be published and that she receive recognition" (p. 17). Setting his writing apart from the work of others, Hemingway encapsulates the story as a fable, a dream narrative in a natural setting, with religious overtones. For Santiago, there will be no "publication" as the marlin is lost to the devouring sharks, only the hard work landing his fish. (The same logic applies to the recovered experiences of "The Snows of Kilimanjaro.")

*The Old Man and the Sea*, as mentioned earlier, was both popular and well received critically, although a minority of reviewers complained that it lacked, as they saw it, Hemingway's usual realism. Did they sense that the novella was artificial and contrived? The standard Hemingway themes are, of course, inscribed in Santiago's story—manhood, courage, a man alone, grace under pressure, etc.—and the story unfolds in a straightforward fashion. Still, one suspects that more is going on. Is the story too personal, too self-reflexive? If so, it would not be the first time that Hemingway had disappointed his readers and critics, nor the first time he played on his readers' misconceptions. Recall the inspired, self-mockery of *Death in the Afternoon*: "what we want in a book by this citizen is people talking; that is all he knows how to do and now he doesn't do it. The fellow is no philosopher, no savant, an incompetent zoologist, he drinks too much and cannot punctuate readily, and now he has stopped writing dialogue. Some one ought to put a stop to him. He is bull crazy" (p. 120). To get at the basis for the discomfort of particular critics, we need to introduce a more complicated framework, one that ties together Hemingway's works, his life as lived, the career carved out of an accumulated series of works and, correspondingly, the Hemingway "text," which is "the increasingly conscious transformation (of the career) into writing."[5]

In an extended discussion of the interrelationship of text and career, Said argues an essential point: "As a definite presence, as positivity, the text occupies a place from which everything else, especially the past, has been crowded out. Yet for the writer the text is also that made thing by virtue of which his career signifies its beginning, its course, and its goal. According to this formulation, then, the text is a pure sign of the writer's career."[6] This perspective on textuality follows from a close reading of Renan's *Life of Jesus*, Freud's *Interpretation of Dreams,* and major modern writers, both literary and philosophical. The upshot of Said's argument is that the traditional configuration of "the author *and* the work" should be replaced by an idea of the text where it is a matter of the writer *in* the work, since "the text is a pure sign of the writer's career." In this sense, Hemingway's text is an achieved hyper-realism and only incidentally concerns the faithful representation of external reality.

Roland Barthes, in *S/Z* and the essays of *Image, Music, Text*, questions that zone where a "work" ends and the "text" begins. The work, with an attached "papa," lives at the expense of the text, whose anonymity knows no end. Inevitably, the text is the linking of individual works but not in a progressive linear development. Rather, it is the writer's beginning intentions that are reexamined at successive stages in the writer's career and repeated with variations. In this sense, as Said writes, a text is "neither a 'creative' masterpiece nor a fact of nature" ... but it is that "which must always be produced constantly."[7] Failed writers—those mentioned for instance in *The Sun Also Rises*—never aspire beyond the "work." Their work reflects and records the pain and drudgery of their personal experience but never the pleasure of the text. Understandably, a young author produces a work and desires recognition, but he also experiences the pleasure of the text. Like Nick Adams in "Big Two Hearted River," he may abort the text for the security of accomplishment and later, he may find ways to thinly disguise the text as a work, as Hemingway did in *Death in the Afternoon* or *Green Hills of Africa*. Over the long run, the text is not easily repressed by a modern writer, since things "were not so simple" and, in the case of *Death in the Afternoon*, Hemingway's understanding of a fifteen-minute spectacle required 519 pages and endless references to other source books. Even then, "it is not enough of a book" (p. 278). And, given the nature of the text, it is never enough of a book. In much the same way, *A Moveable Feast* maintains, "there is never any end to Paris" because "the memory of any person who has lived in it differs from that of any other" (p. 209).

We have arrived at the end of Hemingway's works and only to find not a work but a text. Without surprise, we observe it emerging from the Gulf Stream, that unending permanence inhabited by all genuine writers, who value, above all, the act of writing—in spite of the fact that "you do something which people do not consider a serious occupation" (*GHA*, p. 149). The text is not to be hurried or confused with the spoils of situations. It is not produced by "our good writers" who have reached "a certain age," pressured by external factors, by money, by reputation, or by the desire to write a masterpiece. Nor is the text the product of commercial fishing as described in *The Old Man and the Sea*, where fishing takes place in site of land and the boats are powered by outdoor motors. But the text is less a negation than an affirmation of a process, of a multiplicity, of all that conditions the making of an invisible text. It affirms a productive capability and engenders the work. For this reason it is feminine in its nature; it fascinates and attracts, "so that I was happy as you are after you have been with a woman that you really love . . ." (*GHA*, p. 72), and because *la mar* draws Santiago to his destiny: "He always thought of the sea as *la mar* which is what people call her in Spanish when they love her. Sometimes those who love her say bad things of her but they are always said as though she were a woman. Some of the younger fishermen, those who used buoys as floats for their lines and had motorboats, bought when the shark livers had brought much money, spoke of her as *el mar* which is masculine. They spoke of her as a contestant or a place or even an enemy. But the old man always thought of her as feminine and as something that gave or withheld great favours, and if she did wild or wicked things it was because she could not help them. The moon affects her as it does a woman, he thought" (pp. 29–30). A fascination with procreation is central to the image of *la mar*, as image and as source of the writing career.

*The Old Man and the Sea* is Hemingway's last story and a source for all beginnings. The story could not be simpler, but Hemingway's simplicity should be measured in the context of his remark to Bernard Berenson: "This is the prose that I have been working for all my life and yet have all the dimension of the visible world and the world of man's spirit" (*L*, p. 738). As a modern day saint, Santiago leads us to a secular "unending," which is the text in itself.

5

In early Christianity, the body of the faithful, each and every individual—all of them were known as saints. Miracles were not needed for canonization outside the inaugural miracle of belief itself and a life marked by piety. For early Christians, who lived at the end of time and beyond history, each day was holy. The movement from *For Whom the Bell Tolls* to *The Old Man and the Sea* suggests the same flavor of belief, something on the order of a conversion. Visually, the former novel is shadows and confining spaces that correspond to the negativities of unresolved and irresolvable human passions and wayward actions. But silhouetted against the scenic gloom of dialectics is an unlooked for possibility, where Jordan finds his end with Maria in a sunlit meadow and under an encompassing sky. Here, calculations and mindfulness give way to the quality of sensations and to ever increasing intensities that suggest the existence of a desire beyond desire. Of importance to *The Old Man and the Sea*, the dialectic explored in the Spanish novel collapses not at dusk but noonday, in the dazzling glare of that instant of the shortest shadow.

Santiago, who has lived "a long time," outlasts ordinary human desires. The apotheosis of the last man, he sees all traces of dialectical gloom evaporate in the good weather of September. Everything is as it is, identical to itself: "The sea is the sea. The old man is an old man. The boy is a boy and the fish is a fish. The sharks are all sharks no better and no worse" (*L*, p. 780). Only the sun punctuates this close webbed fabric. It pains Santiago at daybreak, less so at dusk. The marlin is hooked at midday, and, after two days, the fish is landed when "it was not much more than noon" (p. 96). Under the glare of the sun, a spectacle unravels and this spectacle for Hemingway is an interrogation as to "what a man can be," even when the question is answered near the end of his career. In the words of Eliot's "Prufrock," Santiago is given "time for all the work and day of hands/ That lift and drop a question on your plate"—sufficiency in the form of a question.

Why does Santiago continue to fish in old age and why after "he has gone eighty-four days without taking a fish?" Why does he go out so far? How is it that his eyesight is still youthful? Santiago inhabits a cleft between two worlds, almost as if he had died and been allowed to relive his life, returned as himself and another. It is as a new person that he talks aloud at sea, since he knows full well that "it was considered a virtue not to talk unnecessarily at sea" (p. 39). When he speaks to his hand "that was almost as stiff as rigor mortis" (p. 59), it is another who finds voice through him, one who arises out of his loneliness and the division between his earlier and his present self. Santiago regrets having passed beyond ordinary human attachments, but he knows the alternative is demeaning, "first you borrow, then you beg" (p. 18). So he continues to fish because "you have only yourself" (p. 52) and because, as he tells the marlin, "I will show him what a man can do and what a man endures" (p. 62).

Detachment is the precondition of Santiago's strangeness. He is stripped bare of all but the paltriest possessions and his dreams are severely limited. To give himself confidence, he recalls "the great DiMaggio who does all things perfectly even with the pain of the bone spur in his heel" (p. 68). Much is left behind in the experience of old age, but he also happens upon his fortune in his isolation. His reduction of experience opens a realm of untold riches and possibilities that no earlier dream could foretell. The reduction of ordinary experience does not disclose essential poverty but a repopulated existence of mythological dimension, demi-gods and abiding mysteries:

> He looked across the sea and knew how alone he was now. But he could see the prisms in the deep dark water and the line stretching ahead and the strange undulation of the calm. The clouds were building up now for the trade wind and he looked ahead and saw a flight of wild ducks etching themselves against the sky over the water, then blurring, then etching again and he knew no man was ever alone on the sea. (p. 61)

This description, "as good prose as" Hemingway could write, is concrete and, at the same time, abstract and neutral. It seems less a rendering of a scene than a diagram that suggests the forms from which life is multiplied: a prismatic language that breaks down a uniform seascape, the sun's rays into primary colors, the calm surface of the sea that is really a "strange undulation," an etching motion that blurs, "etching again" against the monochrome of a September sky. The most barren seascape begins to reveal not only signs of life that appease the old man's loneliness, but the beginning of life itself.

This sense of the marvelous found in a seemingly prosaic reality informs all aspects of *The Old Man and the Sea*. It sets the stage for Santiago's endurance, his engagement with the marlin, and his first sight of the "great fish":

> The line rose slowly and steadily and then the surface of the ocean bulged ahead of the boat and the fish came out. He came out unendingly . . . and he rose his full length from the water and re-entered it, smoothly. . . . (p. 62)

Santiago's thoughts are completely practical once he sees the marlin, but there is always an air of unreality to his practical concerns when compared to the unending fish. The fact that there are things to be done, if the fish is to be caught, allows Santiago to "integrate" himself. Yet, his activity in no sense exhausts the implications of the scene. Everything regarding the marlin is slightly beyond Santiago (the text is excessive) and beyond his control, its size, its behavior from the time it takes Santiago's bait, and the incomprehensible associations that encompass the struggle. Santiago engages nothing less than the sea, itself, the mysterious *la mar*.

The sea can never be a mere place for work or the drudgery of daily existence. Approached in this fashion, *la mar* repays in kind such that the experience of landing a "great fish" is identified by its market value. In his exhaustion, Santiago, too, computes the value of his fish at 30c/pound, but it is of no consequence. The rules by which he acts do not allow a final mathematical reduction. Rather, due to the form of his experience (and that of career and the nature of the text), he cannot reach the marketplace. What gives the encounter its singular perspective also denies other points of view. At the end, Santiago has only his memory and himself.

An extraordinary fate is given to one who goes out too far to meet his "feminine," one who continues to practice the old ritual forms. Although he distrusts overt religious manifestations, his attitude and conduct are devotional in the same sense that "he was too simple to wonder when he had attained humility" (p. 13). Everything he does with respect to *la mar* manifests a movement beyond worldly concerns. This in no sense implies wishful thinking or slackness of purpose. On the contrary, his devotion is made possible by overcoming the fear and uncertainty that keeps others close to land, in obeying an impulse that tells him that his destiny, and that of "what a man can be," requires that he cross an invisible line—advances out of prosaic existence in a simple yet elevated style. The style is recognizable Hemingway, but it is doubled in motifs only made possible from the perspective of late career.

Having crossed this line—a line made visible in the crossing—the marlin controls the terms of the struggle and draws Santiago further out to sea, beyond sight of land. No landmarks exist for Santiago's experience, no measure for its abnormality. Santiago is powerless to formulate what has happened; he experiences, as did Robert Jordan, the weakness of any language that tries to express the limits and the heights of his being. He is overwhelmed by what surpasses him. Silence is the only adequate response. Repeatedly in Hemingway's works, characters lose control and find themselves overcome by experience, find themselves, through torments and exhaustion, denied their customary security. The oldest possibilities are unhinged by the impossibility of what happens to him in the present. Santiago's transgression in going out too far leads to a more riddling absence:

> And what beat you, he thought.
> "Nothing," he said aloud. "I went out too far." (p. 120)

Santiago's movement out into the Gulf Stream had first passed what "the fishermen called the great well because there was a sudden deep of seven hundred fathoms where all sorts of fish congregated . . ." (p. 28). As he continues outward, he finds the larval forms of life, both "the red sifting of the plankton in the dark water" and "the purple, formalized, iridescent, gelatinous bladder of a Portuguese man-of-war" (p. 35), then flying fish and sea birds—allegories of the first days of Genesis. He has recovered the sea's intrinsic possibilities, the oldest beginnings. (In the same period, Hemingway worked on a book called *The Garden of Eden.*) Returning home, returning to land, this experience is now "nothing," nothing to be seen of what he has experienced other than exhaustion. Even the "great fish" is a skeletal form, a sign of absence. Santiago may escape the negative values of his situation in the present because of his fidelity to the sea and to his ancient practice. His experience, for all that, is simply an index of his isolation in an indifferent world that does not value his particular activity. Santiago is aware of the practices of other fishermen, different from his, but refuses to act in any other way than he does. Nevertheless, following "eighty-four days now without taking a fish," and now having achieved the goal of his meticulous application, with the marlin lashed to the side of his skiff, he no longer feels the "unending" he had first experienced. Immediately, the marlin's lovely colors begin to fade.

The mystery ends with the marlin dead; and the sharks are little more than anticlimax. Santiago has returned to a world of limits and positive constraints. When he wonders if he has committed a sin, he knows that, in one sense or another, he has broken a taboo and knows, because of that, he has returned to a world of limits. The exhaustion of Santiago is unknown to the dialectical imagination, except, perhaps, in the original mastery of the noble. The success of Santiago's action is measured by a dying fall and in the declaration of brotherhood as the marlin dies: "He is my fortune, he thought. But that is not why I wish to feel him. I think I felt his heart" (p. 95). And it is an action related to primitive gestures and earliest festivals where the accumulation of a year's work was extravagantly wasted and the insularity of profane existence was overcome—not without trepidation. With the exception of Manolin, there is no posterity that awaits Hemingway's re-creation. Rather, there is the ironic depreciation in the last lines of the story:

"Tiburon," the waiter said. "Eshark." He was meaning to explain what had happened. "I didn't know sharks had such handsome, beautifully formed tails." (p. 127)

We should not be too hasty in dismissing this accident of language or the similarity of the marlin and the shark in a confusion of *tails*—"beautifully formed" tales.

The sharks are an empty, emptying form of Santiago's story, against which he struggles to the point of exhaustion. Both the marlin and first shark, a "great mako," emerge from the same fabulous and fabulating element, the depths of the Gulf Stream. In addition to their tails, a single trait distinguishes them:

He was a very big Mako shark built to swim as fast as the fastest fish in the sea and everything about him was beautiful except his jaws. His back was as blue as a sword fish's and his belly was silver and his hide was smooth and handsome. He was built as a sword fish except for his huge jaws. . . . This was a fish built to feed on all the fishes of the sea. (pp. 100–101)

This shark is devoted to a single satisfaction, the single truth of his "great jaws." Once he scents the blood of the marlin, he is "absolutely without caution." But the shark's rapaciousness and singleness of "mind" is its undoing. This, too, is a part of the story, of Hemingway's parable of the death, that follows from dedication to a single truth.

Santiago's "great fish" is altogether unbelievable, while no one questions that sharks, whether great or small, are utterly convincing and demystifying. Sharks, in our imagination, are allied with reality so that even Santiago, in his exhaustion, starts to doubt what he has experienced, in the same way that Jordan, before his death, wonders about his last three days. Marlin and shark inhabit the same waters, in spite of the fact that we extend belief to one and not the other. Is the exclusiveness of our belief not conditioned by the fact that the marlin and the shark are known by their respective tales and also by the order of succession in which these stories come to us, that is, from an older to a newer story, from illusion to disillusion?

To the end, Hemingway engaged the specter of decadence and counterpoised the skeletal outline of a simple story of endurance, an archaic stratum against the historical present. In this sense, Santiago's individual fortune is pitted against sharks that attack in bands to satisfy their desire; he contests, as does Hemingway, the decline in the ability to mystify, to fabulate, to produce gods in our time. Nietzsche, who had ample reason to question the intellectual and artistic tendencies of his age, constructed a fable of the sun that he called the "history of an error." His purpose was to show how truth, at noonday, reveals itself as a fable or a lie to which we have extended belief. From that eclipse when Plato ironically devoured Homer, the sun emerges to redress an error of language and the confusion of the marlin's handsome tale. Stories are again possible—might be all there is once we discover the "history of an error." Learning that nothing is more mystifying than demystification, we recover through Hemingway the dimension of the fabulous and the world—pagan and Homeric—"of man's spirit." There is no sadness and no irony in *The Old Man and the Sea*, only the clarity of noonday.

6

In another letter to Bernard Berenson in 1952, Hemingway recounts a telling anecdote: "during the fascist bombing and shelling of Madrid the slogan was for the people who could not read or write, 'Respect anything you do not understand. It may be a work of art.' Seems like a pretty good basic slogan any time" (*L*, p. 791). Further, during periods of decadence, the work of art is incomprehensible. It may be a work that lies shattered in a ruined city, an issue of audience and the "separate peace" mentioned by Nick Adams, who lies wounded in the rubble of a war-torn village. In any case, the work of art, from the standpoint of Hemingway's natural history of the dead, is a ruin. The "great work" belongs to the past: "The unobtainable is something else. The mountains have all been climbed, most countries worth visiting have been explored long ago and in old places like Africa you learn that many people had seen everything long before they were financed by missionary money or James Gordon Bennett" (*L*, p. 837). *Green Hills of Africa* explores Hemingway's substitution for an age of discovery and the recognition that "a continent ages quickly once we come." An alternative for the modern artist, the last undiscovered country, was a life as lived and experienced as the basis of a work. This realignment fates the modern work to a strange destiny, in outlining the artist's eccentric career, an uneven development through the resistances encountered and, with luck and inventiveness, overcome. Displacements and abnegations, the struggle to endure, repetition and innovation, and a dedication to the act of writing and to the always new text that disperses through a long career, even though people "do not think it a serious occupation"—these are the elements inscribed in the artist's endurance.

To identify an artist's life with his work in no sense implies the careless linking of Hemingway's biography with his main protagonists. Hemingway constantly rejected the suspicious digging of his more persistent academic critics: "Criticism is getting all mixed up with a combination of the Junior F.B.I.-men, discards from Freud and Jung and a sort of Columnist peep-hole and missing laundry list school" (*L*, p. 751). He admitted that "every writer is in much of his work" but added that "it is not as simple as all that," especially if a critic is drawn to the apparent autobiographical indiscretions in his novels and short stories: "The other thing that seems incongruous in the thesis that I can only write about myself is: Who then is Francis Macomber? Is that me? I know very well it is not" (*L*, p. 745). The young writer may be his most biographical self in his works, but even so he is himself with respect to the demands of the work of art, pre-existing in himself as "a law of his nature." If Hemingway is in much of his work, it is through characters who explore the situations he felt compelling both for their resonance in his time and for their ability to reflect the ongoing activity of his writing. For example, the first stories and vignettes explore the situation of individuals deprived of belief who feel that life passes them by. Consequently, their attention turns to experimentation with different practices that may counteract the decay of belief and feeling. It is in this way that Hemingway sought a form of writing that intensified reality. Similarly, *The Sun Also Rises*, beyond its more or less superficial construction as a *roman a clef*, plays off Jake Barnes and Robert Cohn in terms of their respective attraction or indifference to the bullfight. At the extreme Jake Barnes rejects novels like W. H. Hudson's *The Purple Land* as "a very sinister book if read too late in life." In the 1930s, Hemingway's most distinctive and lively period, he was indistinguishable from the work of art. Finally, who is Santiago—whose experience was described as a "million dollar postscript" (*L*, p. 758) to a painter's story in *Islands in the Stream*—if not a figure for the artistic reduction of life to its essentials, if not a recapitulation of the conditions that underlie the modern work of art?

A writer's anachronistic position in our time is the basis for Hemingway's works, as the result of the "flattening of value" and the "system of pettiness" of decadent periods. Anachronism is the sign for an activity that sustains its intrinsic worth and self-sufficiency, because the decadent threat to values lies in normalization and systematic rationalization. One way that Hemingway combated the system was to follow the internal dictates of his writing wherever that might lead in the elaboration of the text. This pronounced tendency entailed the parallel recovery of a form of permanence—which, for Hemingway, often assumed an archaic dimension—as an essential aspect of the modern work. His typical experience involves individuals at the limit, exhausted by this experience, who sketch for the moment the outline of a lost continuity and coherence. This process may imply an empty form, but, as an action found in all his works, it also achieves in its crossing an intensity and clarity, the sunshine of noonday. Contravening Benjamin's lament in "The Storyteller," it is always midday for the storyteller, that fabulous and fabulating moment that puts to rest the specter of decadence. Normal communication may have been a casualty of WWI, but in its place there is the possibility of a work of art as a continuous re-beginning.

# Afterword

*To bring into existence and not to judge ... what has value can be made or distinguished only by defying judgment.*

Gilles Deleuze

1

There is nothing strange in the recognition that an artist starts from experience, understood from the point of view of personal experience and historical and artistic settings. That he uses this experience is also untroubling. Complications arise when deciding which experience matters and how it can be used. We know that Hemingway recorded a range of experience in his works, from his earliest personal recollections, through two wars and his involvement in the Spanish Republican cause. Then, the Paris years and "all that world of writing" and the important discovery of bullfighting. In the 1930s, it was the increasingly frequent ordeal of attending to his public and his critical reception and the attention paid to the particularities of career, and so on.

Whatever the experience and the emotions it may have generated, it was a basic determinant of Hemingway's work and "development."

When he states the need to start writing from what you know, he is referring to direct experience. Colonel Cantwell distinguishes a valid recollection from the spurious on the basis of firsthand experience. *To Have and Have Not*, whatever one thinks concerning its success as a novel, develops along the same axis of perception as *Across the River and Into the Trees*. Posited in the novel is the multiplicity of points of view, the direct experiences of multiple characters, against the imagined singular perspective of Richard Gordon, who reduces experience to the ultimately saleable set piece. The portrait of Richard Gordon is Hemingway's *J'accuse* of a particular reading public and a politicized critical apparatus. Experience has become a wedge concept for Hemingway; it distinguishes "true writing" from formulaic writing and all that follows from either orientation.

More generally, the two stories of *To Have and Have Not* counterpoint an experience based on knowledge against one without firsthand background or informed understanding. The differences are telling. Richard Gordon, on the one hand, lives a life of self-involvement and blindness to others. Harry Morgan, on the other hand, reflects actual life as lived, without subterfuge or alibi. In this respect, Harry's life story is an updated version of *Beyond Good and Evil*, actual recorded experiences that exceed traditional categories, moral, political, or artistic. Harry's life as we see in the novel takes unexpected turns, is not easy to characterize, exceeds concepts. Is this because he is an active agent within a flux of forces and is compelled to invent new ways of acting? In this sense, is he another of the Hemingway models for artistic activity?

In the Spanish novel, we find Robert Jordan, who moves behind enemy lines to encounter a life-ending experience, an experience that gains value in exceeding Marxist concepts and theorizing. In *For Whom the Bell Tolls*, power relationships as experienced among the partisans displace political categories, suggesting an advance on the situation of *To Have and Have Not* in the open ground of a free action.

This study has emphasized the many occasions that Hemingway adjusted to changing circumstances. Yet, categorical thought was always an essential target, much in the same way, perhaps, that "the sight of a priest" could stimulate either Goya or Stendhal, "those good anti-clericals into a rage of production" (*DIA*, p. 204). In the

1930s, Hemingway attempted to educate his public, to see things as they are and to change the way one thinks. If he wanted to write "truly," to search and discover the truth, it was because the truth changes what we think, how we think, and quite possibly changes who we are. A difficult goal and, it would appear he was unsuccessful. Yet, it was the problem he set for himself.

*Death in the Afternoon* demonstrates the capacity of experience to change what we are, to alter identities. In going to a bullfight Hemingway had a definable objective. But it was so much more than he had expected and "so far from simple" that it ultimately changed his way of looking at things; as a "true" experience, it exceeded all his expectations. At the same time, in the book that opens that experience to us, the "author" undergoes a marked transformation; a prior identity gives way to a new one—more garrulous, more knowledgeable, and, whatever one might think, more attuned to his artistic, social, and political setting. In short, when he steps beyond his established identity, he gains all that he can be, in spite of the fact that this confounds those who have made their peace with an earlier avatar of the "author." Follow experience and there is no knowing where it leads.

Liz Coates, as the first issue of a modern naturalness in "Up in Michigan," felt "funny" as she gives herself over to a new experience, when she crosses the line between normal behavior and you know what. Jake Barnes finds clarity of purpose after the experience of the bullfight and so, too, Frederic Henry following the Italian retreat. Everything changes in the 1930s, but not the centrality of experience. If Hemingway's early period, in the modernist vein, is a rejection of bourgeois values, the self-certain complacency that masks the neurotic and repressed, the work of the thirties digs deeper through critical evaluations and analysis. The modern is decadent, a flowering at its rottenest point or the "difference of times," as Michel Foucault would say.

It has all changed; "let it all change." Values are relative, except with regard to the individual who makes of his experience a point of honor, who persists in seeing it through even when faced with serious risks. The critical perspective adopted by Hemingway in the 1930s is directed, as always, to preconceptions, to a *common* sense, to those factors that limit life and curtail experience. More than anything, he wishes to understand how things work. It is not the recovery of meaning that goads him. He freely acknowledges that for many the hunt in *Green Hills of Africa* is infantile, "this silliness of kudu," or at the very least is largely viewed as meaningless. But he is interested in how the hunt proceeds, how it works, regardless of its possible reflection on him. For all that, if the experience of the hunt is truthful, it will create correspondences. The openness of other experiences await in the form of Colonel Cantwell and Santiago and they, too, will reflect on career, as they question set identities and other assumptions.

As Deleuze writes, "what has value can be made or distinguished only by defying judgment." The characters of Colonel Cantwell and Santiago go against the grain; they defy judgment. Santiago is judged "*salao*" by his fellow villagers. But Santiago has an experience denied to them. Judgment rests on the presumption of categories and categorical thinking, while experience, by its nature, exceeds categories, always at the limit of what one can know and safely say. With Hemingway we find the uncanny language of experience; it defies judgment and it leads where it leads.

2

Hemingway was always a big, tough guy; he survived two plane crashes, tried his hand, unsuccessfully, at fighting bulls, hunted German submarines in WWII, drank like a maniac, espoused four wives, fished for marlin, hunted large game "under Kilimanjaro." This is reliable information.

In other words, he was not without worldly experience (the list could go on and on). We see some of this aspect of the man in his first two published novels. Jake Barnes is a little skitterish, but tough-skinned nonetheless. Frederic Henry, however, is tough to the bone, sarcastic, self-centered, until a late turning point. Both narrators are worldly wise and only find this knowledge empty. Yet they both possess a knowingness marked by reticence, as part of another general side to things that is the result of an education in a world, that is, the apprenticeship of the artist writing these books. The writer's satisfaction, it is learned and driven home with some degree of pain and anguish, is not that of journalism for Barnes or love and war for Lieutenant Henry. Rather, as Hemingway explicitly states at the beginning of *Death in the Afternoon*, it is about beginning as a writer and, more to the point, discovering the purpose of his writing. Consequently, two new books, as well as many short stories that are intermingled with the books' publications (which can be examined in this light), appear. *Death in the Afternoon* and *Green Hills of Africa* are specifically books devoted to a new and ongoing writer's apprenticeship, the two poles of the modern work of art as seen against the brilliant clarity of an afternoon sun and that of the perils of career that endanger the work of art as seen from Africa.

From the first, it is all about experimenting and learning to be an artist. However, where he attends his earliest stories with silence and his experimentation is solely divulged to close friends—the discussions with Evan Shipman found in *A Moveable Feast* are good examples—now, he produced two books for public reception. In doing so, he knowingly, of course, broke with his earlier practice and created a new face for his public, both factually accurate and partially mythologized. The guiding thread in the new books remains the same as the earliest short stories and novels. It is not simply a matter of the primacy of experience but one's response, immediate and unreflected, not that this immediacy is fully accidental. In some fashion, one must be open to this opportunity, that being the artist's "genius" out of which a new work may arise. One may not know where it leads but impressions, pleasures, and exhilarations point the way. Affects, here, are signposts, and far more certain than worldly approval. Thus, as Hemingway presents the bullfight for his readers, it begins with the emphasis on personally viewing the spectacle and responding to it. The many pleasures of *A Moveable Feast*, written many years later, stem from the same regard for immediate experience as a material event. Sensual and material—these are the elements that take Hemingway away from the disillusionments of worldly doings, society, and all that, wars and so forth, and, to a lesser degree, love. And this is because they point in the direction of the work of art as something more essential, more lasting. Interestingly, these pointers (to the work of art) are found typically, at least for Hemingway, in sports and other trivial pursuits. Again from *A Moveable Feast*, there is the exhilaration of skiing avalanche country: "We loved the Voralberg and we loved Schruns . . . there was a great glacier run, smooth and straight, forever straight if your legs could hold it . . ." And all of *Death in the Afternoon* is testimony to the importance of material sensations, but one finds, indeed, added complications. Clearly, sensations do not stand alone and would be totally confusing without preparation. More to the point, however, the bullfight as a treasure trove of exhilarating sensations is also a particular form of artistic activity with a major drawback: "it is an impermanent art as singing and dancing are, one of those that Leonardo advised men to avoid, and when the performer is gone the art exists only in the memory of those who have seen it and it dies with them." Hemingway explores this thought at length and concludes, "Memory, of course, is never true." Another stage in Hemingway's knowledge has been reached, one that leads back to his own concerns as writer and one that is found in a single phrase in the last chapter of *Death in the Afternoon*: "Make all that come true again" (p. 272). Or more generally: "if you ride and if your memory is good you may ride still through the forest of the Irati with trees like drawings in a child's fairy book" (p. 274). Another contemporaneous example: leaving Africa and Mr. J. P. behind, Pauline is upset that she can't remember his face—"already I can't see him"—and Hemingway speaks up: "'I can remember him,' I said. 'I'll write you a piece some time and put him in'" (p. 295). The writer's role becomes even more defined.

There is a passage in Walter Benjamin's essay on Proust where he identifies Proust's homesickness and his desire for the original, the first happiness. Thus, for Benjamin, the basis for the importance and convolutions he gives to forgetting and remembering in Proust. In certain sections of this book, I have made reference to Proust and it is known that Hemingway read him. What is equally clear are their apparent differences, in terms of background, social standing, style, experiences, and, from a writer's point of view, the organization of their work: dense and closely related volumes for Proust that flow in a particular direction toward "time recaptured" and, in Hemingway's case, disjointed and far more episodic works seemingly lacking purposeful accumulation or end point. This is at best a partial view. Consider an exchange between Robert Jordan and Anselmo in the early sections of *For Whom the Bell Tolls*. Anselmo, proud like all Spaniards, brave and resolute, has given everything for the revolution, and most painful and desolating for him is the loss of old forms ("after all this is over and we have won the war, there must be a penance of some kind for cleansing us all," [p. 196]), and, generally, the loss of spirituality. Jordan can only offer sad comfort from the perspective of dialectics and class struggles until the gift he is given of Maria. Here, he encounters his own secularized form of spirituality, his own version of "for whom the bell tolls" if not for thee. And with this, the elements of an apprenticeship come together in the Spanish novel through an individual and individualizing perspective. Earlier progress is reflected and repeated. A social world and its changing fashions, political programs, love, the natural world, sensations and excitement, and novel experiences—these come together. A whole world has been created in a language that often strains credibility, a distinct, Spanish amalgam that sets it all apart.

A further point requires attention. From the writer's point of view, the objective, in a situation of radical loss—it is total war—is to save all he can and we find this recovery in the education given by Pilar. It is Pilar who shows Jordan how to recapture the past as it dies away, in the moment that it dies, and that is the task of the artist in both Hemingway and Proust. In "The Snows of Kilimanjaro," a writer lies dying, as we all know, and because of his lack of discipline, laziness, he laments the work he failed to do and blames his wife. He drifts off periodically and "writes" the scenes and experiences he had failed to write through his neglect. The writing is saved from death and forgetfulness. At the ending of the story, the writer, in a hallucination, is flown to the top of Kilimanjaro: "Its western summit is called the Masai 'Ngàje Ngài,' the House of God. Close to the western summit there is a dried and frozen carcass of a leopard. No one has explained what the leopard was seeking at that altitude." As for the writer, now dying:

> *And there, ahead, all he could see, as wide as all the world, great, high, and unbelievably white in the sun, was the square of Kilimanjaro. And then he knew that was where he was going.*

# Appendix

## 1. BACKGROUND SKETCHES

*T*hings change and, among Hemingway's major works, no two are alike, whether in subject matter or artistic form, as Michael Reynolds tirelessly repeated. In Hemingway's language it is always a matter of "expediencies." In part, this variety results from "how the world has been," but it is also the product of an evolving career. Given this, the natural tendency is to seek some stability, a reasonable degree of constancy. This has led some critics to look beneath the surface of Hemingway's works to uncover a "code hero," beginning with Frederic Henry, or to find in Hemingway's alleged sexual ambivalence an "open sesame."

There is the possibility, however, for a different working method based on what seems to me is a literate literalness. This leaves a world of surfaces where different works appear different. Historical context, here, would highlight the uneven movement of differences over time. To this end and without attempting to draw out similarities, brief sketches of the works discussed in this study are provided below. Following this are short, personalized summaries of the thought of Michel Foucault, Gilles Deleuze, and Edward Said, the three thinkers who served as signposts in my approach to Hemingway.

# Hemingway Sketches

*In Our Time* (1925)

This first American publication of Hemingway's set the stage for his life-long relationship with Scribner's. The stories and the unusual nature of the collection itself were clearly experimental, but Scribner's accepted the risk of publication based on the promised rights to *The Sun Also Rises* and the urging of Fitzgerald, one of Scribner's most successful authors.

The subject of the stories varies widely, from "native" pieces such as "Indian Camp," "The Three-Day Blow," and "Big Two Hearted River," where one finds the "budding artist" in the character of Nick Adams, to other stories that appear to stand by themselves, "My Old Man," "The Battler," "Cat in the Rain," and "Out of Season." In addition, many of the stories deal with WWI and its aftereffects. Further, the collection contains inter-chapters ("vignettes") inserted between each of the stories, some of which had appeared earlier in avant-garde magazines. Very short pieces, the inter-chapters largely focus on battle scenes and bullfighting.

The last three give a good sense of Hemingway's interest. Chapter 14 ends the bullfighting sequence with the death of Maera: "Once the horn went all the way through him and he felt it go into the sand" (p. 207). Following this is the hanging of Sam Cardinella, an awful affair: "When they came toward him with the cap to go over his head Sam Cardinella lost control of his sphincter muscle. The guards who had been holding him up both dropped him" (p. 219). Finally, "L'Envoi" presents a king "working in his garden," of whom it is said—the last words of *In Our Time*—"It was very jolly. We talked for a long time. Like all Greeks he wanted to go to America" (p. 233). These short scenes are intended to play against each other and to create a broad context of in our time. Equally suggestive, these last inter-chapters bracket parts 1 and 2 of "Big Two-Hearted River."

*The Sun Also Rises* (1926)

This may be Hemingway's most popular novel; it undoubtedly became a cult classic, creating a July exodus of college students to the

"Feria of San Fermin" at Pamplona for the "running of the bulls." Tourist maps of the Paris bar scene can be had that trace the night-time meanderings of Jake Barnes's expatriate crowd.

The novel, originally called *Fiesta*, centers on Jake Barnes, a newsman living in Paris after WWI. He has suffered a debilitating "wound" in the war and gains what pleasure he can in his work, his friendships, and his avocation as an *aficionado* of the bullfight. At the beginning of the book a number of characters are introduced, most important, Bret Ashley, the "love interest," and Robert Cohn. The back and forth of this love triangle is developed and ultimately pushed to the side when Jake Barnes meets up with Bill Gorton, an old friend and practicing writer. They head for Spain, while Brett and Robert go off to San Sebastian. The two friends spend time trout fishing in Spain and then arrive at Pamplona for the "fiesta," a period of drunken revelry. Brett and Robert Cohn meet up with Jake and other friends. The novel's ending is memorable:

> "Oh Jake," Brett said, "we could have had such a damned good time together."
>
> . . . .
>
> "Yes," I said. "Isn't it pretty to think so."

Of particular interest, of course, are the scenes at the end of the novel that show the bullfight and the exciting competition between Belmonte, who had come out of retirement, and Romero, a bullfighter fully in control of his actions: "he let the bull pass so close that the man and the bull were all one sharply etched mass" (p. 217).

## A Farewell to Arms (1929)

The main character of this novel is Frederic Henry. Partially reflecting Hemingway's Italian experience in WWI, Henry is an ambulance driver who is injured at the front and sent to a hospital in Milan. In the first of five "books," Henry meets Catherine Barkley, an English nurse, and begins to show an interest in her (not quite a traditional courtship). In book 2, Henry is recuperating in Milan and meets up again with Catherine; they fall in love. By the end of book 2, Catherine is three months pregnant. Henry returns to the front (book 3), when the

Austro-German forces attack, which leads to the retreat of the Italian troops. A decisive scene, here, involves Henry's escape from the "battle police" who are executing, indiscriminately, officers of the retreating forces. In the last two books, Frederic Henry and Catherine reunite and run off to Switzerland. Their son and Catherine die in childbirth. Frederic Henry, at the end of the novel, is left by himself: "'No,' I said, 'there is nothing to say'" (p. 332). The novel ends.

As a skeleton of a serious literary work, this description does little to suggest the cumulative impact of the novel, the interplay of characters, the emotional intensity, and the new experience that follows WWI. The novel firmly established Hemingway's reputation, his recognizable style, and a firm grounding for an evolving career. For many readers, it is still seen as one of the two or three best novels to come out of WWI. It engages historical and intellectual issues of the first importance.

### Death in the Afternoon (1932)

Considerable detail concerning this work can be found in chapter 3 of this study. It might be useful, nevertheless, to highlight other obvious facts. First, although Hemingway writes in the last chapter of the book (chapter 20) "if I could have made this enough of a book it would have had everything in it" (p. 270), it does contain far more material than chapter 3 would lead the reader to think. It includes 129 pages of illustrations, 87 pages given to "An Explanatory Glossary" (with the accurate drawings of such things as the "*vara*: shaft; pic used in bullfighting"). And these entries are inclusive; as an example, the glossary ends with this last notation: "*Zapatillas*: heel-less pumps worn by bullfighters in the ring." After the glossary, there is a section called "Some Reactions of a Few Individuals to the Integral Spanish Bullfight," followed by four pages that reviews the performance of Sidney Franklin, the American matador, nine pages on "Dates of Bullfights," and a closing "Bibliographical Note." This entry concludes that "the present volume, *Death in the Afternoon*, is not intended to be either historical or exhaustive. It is intended as an introduction to the modern Spanish bullfight and attempts to explain that spectacle both emotionally and practically. It was written because there was no book which did this in Spanish or in English" (p. 519).

*Green Hills of Africa* (1935)

Hemingway and his second wife, Pauline Pfeiffer, went to East Africa on safari in December 1933. The recounting of this experience in this "nonfiction" work is organized in four parts. The section headings that introduce each part are self-explanatory: part 1—"Pursuit and Conversation"; part 2—"Pursuit Remembered"; part 3—"Pursuit and Failure"; part 4—"Pursuit as Happiness." The hunt, of course, is eventful with detailed descriptions and personal reflection on the events that occur. Reminiscences play a part at the end of a day's hunt, while having a drink before dinner, or when there is an interruption in the hunt itself. The reflections on literature are well known and prized as revealing Hemingway's seriousness with respect to his craft and career. The safari ends, "Pursuit as Happiness," with a successful and intense sequence in which Hemingway finally "bags" his kudu in wonderful country. But there is, of course, the disappointment of returning to camp to learn that Karl, Hemingway's friend, has shot an even bigger trophy kudu.

Remarkable is the novelty of this work when seen in the context of his earlier production. It is neither "a work of the imagination" nor a transparent, discursive elaboration of personal interests (i.e., the bullfight). It is new and unexpected writing and attempts "to see whether the shape of a country and the pattern of a month's action, if truly presented" can equal in quality and "truthfulness" the effect of his novels. In none of his major writing does Hemingway repeat himself; the setting is different, the experience different, and, always, there are new beginnings.

*To Have and Have Not* (1937)

This book is another of Hemingway's "novels" constructed from short stories, three stories in this instance. "One Trip Across" and "The Tradesman's Return" are the first two stories, retitled "Harry Morgan—Spring" and "Harry Morgan—Fall." Written some time later is "Harry Morgan—Winter," the third story and the longest of the three. While the first two stories highlight Harry Morgan and his increasingly futile and violent attempts to make a living in the Florida Keys during the Great Depression, the last story, "Winter," introduces a great many "extraneous" characters and a decidedly literary cast to the action with the introduction of Richard Gordon.

The opposition of "have" and "have not" fleshes out the characters in the novel; there are rich yachtsmen in Key West, administration officials, a tavern owner—the "haves"—and far more "have nots"—immigrants, revolutionaries, the disenfranchised "vets," Harry Morgan, of course, and Albert, his mate. Economic forces, one way or another, determine the conduct of both the "haves" and the "have nots." The outcome of all this is as one might expect.

*For Whom the Bell Tolls* (1940)

In this novel, Hemingway returned to literary prominence. It tells of another displaced American, who joined the International Brigade to assist the partisan cause during the Spanish civil war. In this sense, it is also about the haves and have nots, only now on a far larger canvas of geopolitical import.

Robert Jordan, the novel's narrator and main protagonist, has the mission to destroy a critical bridge behind enemy lines, before a major Republican offensive. The action takes place over a three-day period and includes personal flashbacks and earlier dealings with the Russian cadre in Madrid. With the small band of partisans, his first objective is to gain their assistance, especially that of their leader, Pablo, who resists Jordan's plan. When Pablo is replaced as leader by Pilar, Jordan's plan is enacted and the bridge blown. However, the general offensive has been betrayed. No observable gain is achieved by Jordan's action in the larger framework and he is crippled when escaping from an advancing fascist militia troop. At the end of the story, he is lying on a hillside awaiting his fate while the partisans ride off.

Woven into this story is Jordan's brief love affair with a young woman, Maria, who has suffered at the hands of the fascists. Their love is instantaneous and all consuming; it questions Jordan's training and indoctrination in the new politics of the Republican cause. The novel's intense action involves both a practical mission and an experience that goes beyond the ordinary.

The film version of the novel (1943) starred Gary Cooper, a friend of Hemingway's from Sun Valley, and Ingrid Bergman. It was nominated for nine Academy Awards.

*Across the River And Into the Trees* (1950)

In the ten years since his last novel, Hemingway published very little, but, after WWII, he gave himself to his writing in an obsessive fashion. Much of this work he did not publish. Of the two works that were published out of this intense effort after the war, this novel was the first to appear.

It recounts the last days of a dying soldier, Colonel Richard Cantwell, in Venice. The novel begins with the scene of duck hunting in the Venetian canals and follows with Cantwell's residence at the Gritti Hotel, where he meets with Renata, another excessive love interest. Urged by Renata, Cantwell recalls personal war experiences and records his judgment of the Allied commanders, Eisenhower, Patton, Montgomery, and others. He is bitter. In the backseat of his staff car, returning to base, he dies of a heart attack.

*The Old Man and the Sea* (1952)

This work was originally intended as a postscript to *Islands in the Stream* and it is said to be the basis for Hemingway's award of the Nobel Prize. It has no chapters or parts and develops as a complete, uninterrupted story—an old man, Santiago, sets out to sea from Cuba in a small skiff, goes out further and further, hooks a giant fish, plays the fish to exhaustion, lands the fish, lashes it to his skiff. As a coda, a great mako shark attacks the marlin, is beaten off and killed, but other sharks appear and finish the mako's devastation. The old man returns to shore without his prize. End of story, except for the tourist couple who observe the marlin's carcass and, mistaking a Spanish word, believe Santiago's fish to be a shark.

*A Moveable Feast* (posthumous publication, 1964)

From San Francisco de Paula, Cuba, in 1960, Hemingway wrote: "If the reader prefers, this book may be regarded a fiction." It is, of course, Hemingway's portrait of the artist as a young man. It covers a wide range of topics, from gambling, horse racing, involvement with little magazines and contemporaries, his judgments, his dedication to writing, friendships with Fitzgerald and Sylvia Beach. There is so much more.

This experience ends with the arrival of "the rich." That is when, four decades later, he remembers the loss caused by that arrival: "When I saw my wife standing by the tracks as the train came in by the piled logs at the station, I wished I had died before I ever loved anyone but her. She was smiling, the sun on her lovely face tanned by the snow and sun, beautifully built, her hair red gold in the sun, grown out all winter awkwardly and beautifully, and Mr. Bumby standing with her, blond and chunky and with winter cheeks looking like a good Vorarlberg boy" (p. 208). But then, "The Sun Also Rises."

## Critical Sketches

In my discussion of *For Whom the Bell Tolls*, I refer to Said's journal article "Secular Criticism" as a critical stance that generously includes both the artist and the literary critic. In the same vein, one finds in "What Is Enlightenment?"—a late essay of Foucault's—the basis for a positive and inclusive critical attitude for both artist and critic. Foucault calls this "the attitude of modernity," the basis for a particular relationship to one's present seen, specifically, as the "will to heroize the present." The work required, Foucault explains, is "to imagine (the present) otherwise than it is, and to transform it not by destroying it but by grasping it in what it is. Baudelairean modernity is an exercise in which extreme attention to what is real is confronted with the practice of a liberty that simultaneously respects this reality and violates it."

The secondary literature on Deleuze, Foucault, and Said is extensive and it has not been my intention to enter into debates about particular works or particular interpretations of their work. In this study, I say little about these thinkers, except for the occasional remark or use of a theoretical point or other. My focus, as they say, has been Hemingway and his works. Yet, it seems fair to admit that the thought and perspectives of these thinkers have influenced my approach far more than that of traditional Hemingway scholars, perhaps because I perceive the latter's work as too closed in on itself. In many ways, Hemingway scholarship is a self-perpetuating machine, whether the scholar resorts to the archive, the endless fascination of close readings, the pleasures of new manuscript material. It's something out of Borges—you could spend your whole life . . .

The idea for this study began with being struck by the possible affinity between "Up in Michigan" and Foucault's "Preface to Transgression." Furthermore, I realized, over time, the central place given to literature in the works of Deleuze, Foucault, and Said, who might be loosely characterized as philosopher, historian, and literary critic/political advocate. If nothing else, their work, when brought to bear on Hemingway, broadens the canvas, forces one's attention to what Foucault had called "exteriority," or the always present "it goes without saying" that determines outcomes. It should also be remembered that, although he has been accused of nihilism, a pointless relativism, his objective, as he stated toward the end of his life, was a "problematization" of his experience, such that present experience could be opened to a new freedom with regard to one's identity, one's thought, and one's actions, without knowing the outcome.

In the short sketches that follow, I try to present a simple overview, with very little in the way of detail. These sketches are meant more as a matter of flavor and possible relevance to Hemingway.

## Gilles Deleuze & Michel Foucault

For much of their professional careers, Deleuze and Foucault were good friends. Both had influential teachers in Georges Canguilhem and Jean Hyppolite, and in 1969, when Deleuze was appointed to the University of Paris VIII at Vincennes, it was Foucault, then director of the Philosophy Department, who hired him. They supported each other's work in review articles and book-length studies. For example, Foucault's "Theatrum Philosophicum," a review of Deleuze's *Difference and Repetition* and *Logic of Sense*, announces, "perhaps one day, this century will be know as Deleuzian" (*LCMP*, p. 165). (It has been said that this statement may have been an inside joke, understandable given their form of thinking.) In a joint interview for *L'Arc* in 1972, Deleuze observed: "Possibly we're in the process of experiencing a new relationship between theory and practice" (*LCMP*, p. 205). For both thinkers, this shift leads in a variety of directions, beginning with a rethinking of the role of the author. In the case of Deleuze, this rethinking occurs in his position as a "philosopher's philosopher," while for Foucault it entails a movement in and out of philosophy—history from a philosophical standpoint and the obverse, philosophy from a historical standpoint.

Both writers were prolific and both extremely reticent with regard to their private lives. In *Negotiations*, Deleuze says: "Academics' lives are seldom interesting." Foucault, for his part, transformed his desire for anonymity into a point of honor and the perpetual basis for philosophical reflection. In the opening remarks of his inaugural lecture at the Collège de France, he quoted Beckett: "What matters who's speaking, someone said, what matters who's speaking." The "late" Deleuze, at the time he began collaborating with Félix Guattari on *Anti-Oedipus*, and the "late" Foucault seemed to have gone separate ways, but for all that the vigor of their relationship made possible a period of heightened creativity.

*Deleuze (1925–1995)*

Deleuze wrote studies, to name but a few, of Spinoza, Hume, Bergson, Nietzsche, and artists such as Proust, Kafka, and Francis Bacon. He wrote on the cinema and produced works of general philosophical importance: "this century will be known as Deleuzian." His early works on Proust and Nietzsche had a major impact in their respective fields. Philosophically, Deleuze's main problem was the concepts of identity and representation and the attempt to develop a perspective on "difference" in itself, "to grasp beings exactly as they are." Without the occlusion of unifying concepts (examples: space and time), difference, it is argued, is the actuality of existence, the bedrock of experience that conditions new ways of thinking.

According to Deleuze, the traditional "image of thought" derives from *common* sense and what has been presupposed since Plato as a natural desire for truth. Deleuze's view, borrowed in part from Nietzsche, is that thought is a violence done to things and, furthermore, a rupture of established categories, because "truth" changes what we think. Thus, in reading earlier philosophers, Deleuze does not attempt to provide the meaning that engenders a philosophical position. Rather, his concern is to reveal the problem(s) that a system of thought addressed. Much the same approach is found in Deleuze's studies of Proust or Kafka; what problem do they deal with? For Proust, it is an education to the signifying nature of experience as it brings him to a recognition of his vocation and why art, and only authentic art, knits together the differences he has experienced in life.

The late Deleuze, after *Anti-Oedipus*, continues to exhibit a wide range of intellectual interests with his focus on creativity, whether in the philosopher's ability to create concepts or in the work of scientists and artists, such as Francis Bacon. In these circumstanced worlds, it is, inevitably, a matter of going as far as one can to realize a potentiality.

## *Foucault* (1926–1984)

Foucault was always a vagabond, what Deleuze would call "nomadic." He spent several years in Sweden, where much of *Madness and Civilization* was written, in Tunis, at UC Berkeley, Brazil, Japan. His writings were equally peripatetic and included historical studies of madness and the birth of the clinic, a monograph on the writing techniques of Raymond Roussel, an archaeology of the human sciences, a history of the birth of the prison, a projected six-volume study of the history of sexuality, and the last two books with a new focus on Greek and Roman antiquity—an exhausting itinerary. But there is far more, in interviews, articles, and lectures and public activity. In fact, Foucault, given the immense amount of work he accomplished, was extremely generous with his time, offering lucid, modest explanations of his accomplishments. The participants at a conference organized by the "Michel Foucault Centre" in 1989, after his death, attest to the debt many felt in his absence. At that event, even Georges Canguilhem, one of his best teachers, commented on Foucault's "nonconformist attitude" concerning "traditional notions like normality, morality, transgression, and regulation." As Canguilhem summarized Foucault's legacy, his purpose was not to "legitimize what we already know," but to "find out in what way and to what extent it would be possible to think differently."

Without going into any detail concerning the concepts that Canguilhem alludes to (this is, after all, a sketch), it might be helpful to bring up the question of history as it served Foucault's purpose. Many of his works, he has said, begin with a perception, an uncomfortable feeling, about his present circumstances. Something rang false. From this sense of his present, as he writes in "Nietzsche, Genealogy, History," his work began: "Genealogy, consequently, requires patience and a knowledge of details and it depends on a vast accumulation of source material. . . . It cannot be the product of 'large and well-meaning errors.' In short, genealogy demands relentless erudition" (*LCMP*, p. 140). Resulting from Foucault's erudition is a break with a humanist tradition, and also the central role of the subject in "making of history." (In an indirect fashion, existentialism and phenomenology were Foucault's first targets. However, in the last years of his life, he returned to the question of the subject in his examination of ancient ethics and morality, but now free of metaphysical constraints.) As for history (or genealogy), it has a special use in showing that arbitrary elements of the past are still at work, through repeated use, in the present as those things we take for granted. Consequently, the present is revealed as fragile and changeable, thus, as an opportunity for change and free action. The notions of delinquency, normalization, etc., come to us from the past, and we experience their effects but also their weaknesses as compelling forces.

Foucault developed his ideas of discursive regularities, bio-power, confessional technology, the relation of power and truth, and much more from historical insights. Whether known as genealogy or archaeology, Foucault's histories are undoubtedly "nonconformist" and outline how it is that one operates at the limit of what one can think.

Who, then, is Foucault? He has no name, but, if a name is needed, it can be found in an interview with *Le Monde* in 1980 where he referred to himself as "The Masked Philosopher." When asked why he had chosen anonymity, he said: "Out of nostalgia for a time when, being quite unknown, what I said had some chance of being heard. With the potential reader the surface of contact was unrippled. The effects of the book might land in unexpected places and form shapes that I never thought of. A name makes reading too easy."

*Edward Said* (1935–2003)

Following the publication of *Beginnings* and before *Orientalism*, Said's most provocative publication, appeared, he was interviewed by *Diacritics* (Fall, 1976). The exchange begins with Said's discussion of Harold Bloom and his "radical" views on poetic influence. Said was admiring of Bloom's thought but also spoke of his reservations with the thesis of a "heroic" poet who struggles against a dominant predecessor: "Bloom's theory of poetic transmission conceals, I think, a radically mythologized conception of individual determinants of culture, and a total disregard for culture's anonymous and institutional supports, which go on and on beyond individual efforts and life-spans." In addition, Said brings up an obvious but telling point: "Certainly the romantics were aware of Milton, but they were vitally involved also in the journals, reviews, and competing discourses of their time," which Said goes on to summarize as "*the materially productive agencies of the culture* [emphasis mine] that contains, and enables, the romantic poet" (p. 34).

*Orientalism* is, of course, a politically charged analysis, but it is, as well, a work that broadens our understanding of the "material" forces at play in the production of texts. Said's background as a Palestinian, his academic training, his institutional prominence, and his admiration for French thinkers like Foucault—all of this bears on a particular production and the renewed process called "beginnings." Far more explicit in laying out Said's intellectual debts and critical understanding is *Beginnings: Intention and Method,* an important work for my approach to Hemingway. Like Foucault's works, it is a book charged with a sense of present circumstances and the desire to come to terms in the most productive manner with the positive aspects of the present. It is fully conscious of the burden, and also the marginality, that one finds in attempting useful critical work. It brings to bear historical sense, both with regard to the current position of criticism and the shifting sands of what is often referred to as "primary texts." Thus novels and a succession of novelists are shown to have a history and patrimony that wears thin over time. In his chapter on modernist writers and their self-conscious careers, we find the extent to which the act of writing, itself, not only turns inward but has the potential to brutalize the novelist as an empirical being. Subsequently, a key chapter concerns Said's introduction of what was then called "structuralist" writers to an American public, followed by a concluding chapter on Vico's *New Science* (1744), an especially important document for Said. All of it is energetic and enervating and all of it was an artful corrective to the complacencies of critical practices in his time.

## 2. RECENT HEMINGWAY CRITICISM

Scholarly work devoted to Hemingway abounds. My purpose in this brief review of the last few years of Hemingway scholarship is to afford the reader with general information on the current direction in Hemingway studies and, to some extent, to highlight the works that seem to give a renewed force to the "return to Hemingway."

For a general orientation, two earlier reference works are noteworthy in setting the stage: Kelli A. Larson's *Ernest Hemingway: A Reference Guide, 1974–1989* (Boston: G. K. Hall, 1991) and Miriam Mandel's *Reading Hemingway: The Facts in the Fictions* (Lanham, MD: University Press of America, 1995). Of more recent interest are the annotated entries in *American Literary Scholarship*, general editors, David J. Nordloh and Gary Scharnhorst (Raleigh-Durham, NC: Duke University Press). The section editors for "Fitzgerald and Hemingway," Hilary K. Justice and Robert W. Trogdon, observe that in the publications of 2004, "no major theme, method, or critical approach dominated Hemingway studies" (p. 201). For the publication year 2005, they remark that the critical focus "tended toward the 1920s and 1930s, possibly heralding a change from previous years' focus on later works." This seems a significant shift from the posthumous writing to other preoccupations as seen below.

Of note is *Ernest Hemingway: A Literary Reference*, ed. Robert W. Trogdon (New York: Carrol & Graf, 2002). Kim Moreland, reviewing the book in the *Hemingway Review* (23.1, 2003), observes: "Trogdon has created a fascinating book in which Hemingway's voice and those of his critics, reviewers, colleagues, friends, and family are ingeniously placed into fruitful conversation . . . [it] offers insights into that life and writing akin to—and in some ways superior to—those afforded by biography, a remarkable achievement that deserves widespread attention." Also important, according to the editors, was Ronald Berman's short book *Modernity and Progress: Fitzgerald, Hemingway, Orwell* (Tuscaloosa: University of Alabama Press, 2007), offering fresh insights and a new perspective. Another new departure was *A Companion to Hemingway's* Death in the Afternoon, ed. Miriam Mandel (Rochester, NY: Camden House, 2004), a collection of twelve essays; it is the first book-length study of a work of nonfiction by Hemingway. *Under Kilimanjaro*, eds. Robert W. Lewis and

Robert E. Fleming (Kent, OH: Kent State University Press, 2005) was, equally, an important event for Hemingway scholars. With considerable care and knowledge, it revises and expands on the original version of *True at First Light*, ed. Patrick Hemingway (New York: Scribner's, 1999). No pattern evolves out of this work, but it is serious work and worthy of attention.

*Hemingway and the Mechanism of Fame*, ed. Matthew J. Bruccoli with Judith Baughman (Columbia: South Carolina University Press) was released in 2006. It presents a wide range of Hemingway's public utterances: reviews, blurbs, endorsements, public letters. David M. Earle, in the *Hemingway Review* (25.2, Spring, 2006), has an interesting observation on this book and, from my point of view, on the institutional constraints that undoubtedly regulate Hemingway scholarship: "Bruccoli acknowledges his indebtedness to John Raeburn's *Fame Became Him* (1984), still the single best monograph on the construction of Hemingway's public persona. The fact that Raeburn's excellent book did not spark more studies of Hemingway's reputation is a testament to the deeply entrenched academic idea that modernism is separate from the marketplace." In the same vein as Raeburn, Robert W. Trogdon's *The Lousy Racket: Hemingway, Scribners, and the Business of Literature* (Kent, OH: Kent State University Press, 2007) expands the critic's understanding of Hemingway. These last two books demonstrate that it is possible to broaden one's approach; new subject matter and new perspectives now seem possible. Equally useful in this respect is an earlier essay of Susan F. Beegle, "Conclusion: The Critical Reputation," in *The Cambridge Companion to Hemingway*, ed. Scott Donaldson (Cambridge: Cambridge University Press, 1996); it analyzes academic criticism of Hemingway over time and the development of critical consensus.

Of considerable interest to anyone working on Hemingway is the first volume of the *Cambridge Edition of the Letters of Ernest Hemingway*, general editor Sandra Spanier and head of the editorial review board Linda Patterson Miller (Cambridge: Cambridge University Press), forthcoming in 2011. Supported by the Hemingway Society, a fourteen-year project is planned, with the goal of publishing over a dozen volumes, all of the available Hemingway letters, estimated at six thousand to seven thousand. The *Selected Letters* edited by Carlos Baker have been useful in my understanding of Hemingway; imagine the possibilities for further redefinition once the "complete" letters are made available. The Hemingway Society also sponsors the "Annual Hemingway Conference." The next conference is scheduled to take place in Lausanne, Switzerland, in 2010 and its "call for papers" involves "Hemingway's Extreme Geography," with separate sections devoted to (1) geographical places, (2) internal geographies, (3) the space identity (gender, racial, public), and (4) other issues (the extremes of reception, existentialism and mysticism, and the crisis of reality, as examples).

Finally, the *Hemingway Review*, also an undertaking of the Hemingway Society, is published biannually and contains articles, book reviews, and bibliographic entries. Among the major publishers of Hemingway material are the Cambridge University Press (in its "Companion" series and the "Letters Project") and the Kent State University Press. The latter is developing a new series under the heading of "Reading Ernest Hemingway's" . . . novels and short stories. These readings, according to the press Web site, will provide "close line-by-line annotations of and commentaries on Ernest Hemingway's major works . . . and provide guidance for a wide variety of readers."

# Notes

## INTRODUCTION

1. Edmund Wilson, *The Wound and the Bow: Seven Studies in Literature* (Cambridge, MA: Riverside Press, 1941) and Maxwell Geismar, *Writers in Crisis: The American Novel, 1925–1940* (New York: Houghton Mifflin, 1942). A more detailed and, from Hemingway's standpoint, more contentious psychoanalytic reading is found in Philip Young, *Ernest Hemingway* (New York: Rinehart, 1952).

2. Michel Foucault, "Critical Theory/Intellectual History" in *Michel Foucault: Politics, Philosophy, Culture: Interviews and Other Writings, 1977–1984*, ed. Lawrence D. Kritzman (New York: Routledge, 1988), pp. 35–36.

3. Roland Barthes, "Les Sorties du Texte" in *Bataille*, ed. Philipe Sollers (Paris: UGE, 1973), argues that decadence and a corresponding "progressionist regret" is fundamental to the thought of Marx, Nietzsche, and Bataille.

4. Cited by Kenneth S. Lynn, *Hemingway* (Cambridge: Harvard University Press, 1987), p. 411.

5. Michel Foucault, "Fantasia of the Library" in *Language, Counter-Memory, Practice: Selected Essays and Interviews*, ed. Donald F. Bouchard, trans. Donald F. Bouchard and Sherry Simon (Ithaca, NY: Cornell University Press, 1977), pp. 92–93. Subsequent references will be to *LCP*.

6. See particularly "Preface to Transgression," *LCP*, pp. 29–52. For background on "power relations" see *Essential Works of Michel Foucault:*

*Power*, Volume Three, ed. James D. Faubion, trans. Robert Hurley and others (New York: New Press, 2000).

7. Gilles Deleuze, *Proust & Signs: The Complete Text*, trans. Richard Howard (Minneapolis: University of Minnesota Press, 2000) and *Kafka: Toward a Minor Literature* (Minneapolis: University of Minnesota Press, 1986). See also Reidar Due, *Deleuze* (Cambridge: Polity Press, 2007) for a clear analysis of Deleuze's often difficult thought, especially "Cultural Semiotics," ch. 2, pp. 57–76.

8. Due, *Deleuze*, p. 73.

9. Edward Said, *Beginnings: Intention and Method* (Baltimore: Johns Hopkins University Press, 1975), p. 258.

10. See Karlis Racevskis, *Postmodernism and the Search for Enlightenment* (Charlottesville: University Press of Virginia, 1993) for a broad perspective on Foucault's relevance to contemporary academic and political issues.

11. *LCP*, p. 208.

12. *Michel Foucault: Politics, Philosophy, Culture*, p. 326.


# CHAPTER 1

1. Hemingway was likely thinking about Fitzgerald. See *The Crack Up*, ed. Edmund Wilson (New York: New Directions, 1954).

2. See Michel Foucault, *The Archaeology of Knowledge* (New York: Pantheon Books, 1972): "the analysis of discourse . . . does not reveal the universality of a meaning, but brings to light the action of imposed rarity, with a fundamental power of affirmation," p. 234.

3. Walter Benjamin, "The Storyteller" in *Illuminations* (New York: Shocken Books, 1976), p. 84.

4. Said argues that to begin to write it is necessary "to signify and dedicate the redirection of human energy from 'the world' to the page." p. 24.

5. Samuel Beckett, *Proust* (New York: Grove Press, 1931), p. 47.

6. Gilles Deleuze, *Proust & Signs: The Complete Text*, trans. Richard Howard (Minneapolis: University of Minnesota Press, 2000), p. 6.

7. Beckett, *Proust*, p. 64.

8. Ibid.

9. Earl Rovit, *Ernest Hemingway* (Boston: G. K. Hall, 1963), p. 60.

10. "Preface to Transgression" in *LCP*, p. 49.

11. Vincent Descombes, *Modern French Philosophy*, trans. L. Scott-Fox and J. M. Harding (Cambridge: Cambridge University Press, 1980), p. 112.

12. Michel Foucault, *The Order of Things* (New York: Pantheon Books, 1970), p. 300.

13. On Stein's influence, see Arthur Waldorn, *A Reader's Guide to Ernest Hemingway* (New York: Octagon Books, 1981), p. 30.

14. "Preface to Transgression" in *LCP*, p. 30.

15. Paul H. Fry, "The Image of Walter Benjamin," *Raritan* 2, no. 4 (Spring 1983): 51.

16. "Preface to Transgression," in *LCP*, p. 51.

# CHAPTER 2

1. John Rajchman, *Michel Foucault: The Freedom of Philosophy* (New York: Columbia University Press, 1985), p. 17. In his first chapter, "The Ends of Modernism," Rajchman provides a rounded discussion on Continental perspectives of modernism, with a focus on Foucault and other French thinkers.

2. Ibid., p. 18.

3. Ronald Lajoie and Sally Lentz in "Is Jake Barnes Waiting?" *Fitzgerald/Hemingway Annual* (1975), pp. 229–33, identified the "wonderful story" as A. E. W. Mason's "The Crystal Trench" in *The Four Corners of the World* (New York: Scribner's, 1917).

4. Morse Peckham, "Ernest Hemingway: Sexual Themes in His Writing," *Romanticism and Behavior* (Columbia: University of South Carolina Press, 1976), p. 144.

5. Rajchman, *Michel Foucault*, p. 22.

6. *MF*, pp. 107–12.

7. Cited by Carlos Baker, *Hemingway: The Writer as Artist* (Princeton, NJ: Princeton University Press, 1973), p. 86.

8. In a letter to Bernard Berenson, Hemingway wrote: "I always joke and much of it is gallow's humor. You must truly know that no matter how stupid people act, in order not to argue with fools, any writer that you respect at all, or that has given you pleasure, can think a little bit" (*L*, p. 808).

9. Cited by Hannah Arendt in "Introduction," *Illuminations* (New York: Shocken Books, 1976), p. 15; cf., Terry Eagleton, *Walter Benjamin* (London: NLF, 1981), p. 63.

10. Reidar Due, *Deleuze* (Cambridge: Polity Press, 2007), p. 73.

11. Edward Said, *Beginnings: Intention and Method* (Baltimore: Johns Hopkins University Press, 1975), p. 228.

12. Michael Reynolds, *Hemingway's First War: The Making of A Farewell to Arms* (Princeton, NJ: Princeton University Press), p. 281.

13. Ibid., p. 42.

14. James Dawes, *The Language of War* (Cambridge: Harvard University Press, 2002), p. 129.

## CHAPTER 3

1. Carlos Baker, *Hemingway: The Writer as Artist* (Princeton, NJ: Princeton University Press, 1972), pp. 142, 148.

2. Arthur Waldorn, *A Reader's Guide to Ernest Hemingway* (New York: Octagon Books, 1981), pp. 132, 135.

3. Earl Rovit, *Ernest Hemingway* (Boston: G. K. Hall, 1963), pp. 67–77.

4. Baker, *Hemingway: The Writer as Artist*, p. 149.

5. Rovit, *Ernest Hemingway*, p. 27.

6. Richard Gilman, *Decadence: The Strange Life of an Epithet* (New York: Farrar, Strauss and Giroux, 1980).

7. See Foucault, "Nietzsche, Genealogy, History" in *LCP*, pp. 148–49.

8. *Aesthetics and Politics*, trans. Ronald Taylor (London: NLB, 1977), p. 84.

9. Ibid., p. 97.

10. Ibid., p. 85.

11. "Leçon," *October*, no. 8 (Spring 1979): 15.

12. *Aesthetics and Politics*, p. 95.

13. *Dear Scott/Dear Max: The Fitzgerald-Perkins Correspondences*, ed. John Kuckl and Jackson R. Bryer (New York: Scribner's, 1971), p. 175.

14. See George Bataille, *L'érotisme* (Paris: UGE, 1957), "Conclusion."

15. Ibid.

16. *The Order of Things* (New York: Pantheon Books, 1970), p. 300.

17. Nietzsche, *The Gay Science*, # 109.

18. *The Archaeology of Knowledge* (New York: Pantheon Books, 1978), p. 120.

19. "Language to Infinity" in *LCP*, pp. 53–56.

## CHAPTER 4

1. *Hemingway: The Critical Heritage*, ed. Jeffrey Meyers (London: Routledge, 1982), pp. 168–69.

2. Ibid., p. 172.

3. Ibid., p. 176.

4. *Papa: A Personal Memoir* (Boston: Houghton Mifflin, 1976), pp. 22–23.

5. *Dear Scott/Dear Max: The Fitzgerald-Perkins Correspondences*, ed. John Kuckl and Jackson R. Bryer (New York: Scribner's, 1971), p. 131.

Advising Perkins on how to handle Hemingway, Fitzgerald says "he knows nothing of publishing except in the cucoo magazines."

6. Edward Said, *Beginnings: Intention and Method* (Baltimore: Johns Hopkins University Press, 1975), p. 226.

7. Ibid., p. 228.

8. *Hemingway: The Critical Heritage*, p. 219.

9. See Richard Ellman, *James Joyce* (New York: Oxford University Press, 1959), p. 676, for an accurate rendering of the phrase. See also *L*, p. 874n.

10. See Terry Eagleton, *Walter Benjamin* (London: NLF, 1981), p. 59, for an understanding of "The Destructive Character."

11. Said, *Beginnings*, p. 243.

12. Cited by Kenneth S. Lynn, *Hemingway* (Cambridge: Harvard University Press, 1987), p. 415.

13. Marcel Proust, "Time Regained," Vol. VI, in *In Search of Lost Time*, trans. Andreas Mayor and Terrence Kilmartin, rev. D. J. Enright (New York: Modern Library, 2003), pp. 276–80.

## CHAPTER 5

1. Edward Said, *Beginnings: Intention and Method* (Baltimore: Johns Hopkins University Press, 1975), p. 257.

2. Ibid., p. 227.

3. Ibid., p. 254.

4. Ibid., p. 251.

5. Neitzsche, *The Geneaology of Morals*, III, #25.

6. Paul de Man, *Blindness and Insight* (New York: Oxford University Press, 1971), p. 147.

7. Earl Rovit, *Ernest Hemingway* (Boston: G. K. Hall, 1963), pp. 38–39.

8. Reidar Due, *Deleuze* (Cambridge: Polity Press, 2007), p. 58.

9. Ibid., p. 61.

10. Carlos Baker, *Hemingway: The Writer as Artist* (Princeton, NJ: Princeton University Press, 1972), p. 206.

## CHAPTER 6

1. Kenneth S. Lynn, *Hemingway* (Cambridge: Harvard University Press, 1987), p. 450.

2. *Dear Scott/Dear Max: The Fitzgerald-Perkins Correspondences*, ed. John Kuckl and Jackson R. Bryer (New York: Scribner's, 1971), p. 266.

3. Lynn, *Hemingway*, pp. 491, 494.

4. *Aesthetics and Politics*, trans. Ronald Taylor (London: NLB, 1977), p. 82.

5. Carlos Baker, *Hemingway: The Writer as Artist* (Princeton, NJ: Princeton University Press, 1972), p. 250.

6. Gilles Deleuze, *Proust & Signs: The Complete Text*, trans. Richard Howard (Minneapolis: University of Minnesota Press, 2000), p. 42.

7. Gilles Deleuze, *Difference and Repetition*, trans. Paul Patton (New York: Columbia University Press, 1994), p. 131.

8. Deleuze, *Proust & Signs*, pp. 95–96.

9. "Truth and Juridical Forms" in *Essential Works of Michel Foucault: Power*, Volume Three, ed. James D. Faubion, trans. Robert Hurley and others (New York: New Press, 2000), p. 12.

10. Edmund Wilson, *To the Finland Station* (Garden City, NY: Doubleday, 1940), p. 228; cf., Vincent Descombes, *Modern French Philosophy*, trans. L. Scott-Fox and J. M. Harding (Cambridge: Cambridge University Press, 1981), pp. 9–16, for an informed discussion of dialectics.

11. *Michel Foucault: Politics, Philosophy, Culture: Interviews and Other Writings, 1977–1984*, ed. Lawrence D. Kritzman (New York: Routledge, 1988), p. 103. See also Deleuze's *Foucault*, pp. 70–76.

12. *Essential Works of Michel Foucault: Power*, pp. 340–41.

13. Ibid., p. 12.

14. Ibid., p. 342.

15. Cited by Baker in *Hemingway: The Writer as Artist*, p. 217.

16. Ibid., pp. 175–76.

17. Cited by David Magarshack in the introduction, Fyodor Dostoyevsky, *The Idiot*, trans. David Magarshack (New York: Penguin Books, 1981), p. 25.

18. "Secular Criticism," *Raritan* 2, no. 3 (Winter 1983): 12.

19. Ibid., p. 14.

20. Michael Reynolds, *Hemingway's First War: The Making of* A Farewell to Arms (Princeton, NJ: Princeton University Press), p. 129.

# CONCLUSION

1. Rose Marie Burwell, *Hemingway: The Postwar Years and the Posthumous Novels* (Cambridge: Cambridge University Press, 1996), p. 1.

2. Edward Said, *Beginnings: Intention and Method* (Baltimore: Johns Hopkins University Press, 1975), p. 260.

3. Ibid., pp. 261–62.

4. Ibid., p. 263.

5. Ibid., p. 196.

6. Ibid., p. 223.

7. Ibid., p. 197.

# Bibliography

Baker, Carlos. *Hemingway: The Writer as Artist*. Princeton, NJ: Princeton University Press, 1972.

Barthes, Roland. "Leçon." *October*, no. 8 (Spring, 1979).

———. "Les Sorties du Texte." *Bataille*. Ed. Philipe Sollers. Paris: U.G.E., 1973.

Bataille, Georges. *L'érotisme*. Paris: U.G.E., 1957.

Beckett, Samuel. *Proust*. New York: Grove Press, 1931.

Benjamin, Walter. *Illuminations*. New York: Shocken Books, 1976.

Burwell, Rose Marie. *Hemingway: The Postwar Years and the Posthumous Novels*. New York: Cambridge University Press, 1996.

Dawes, James. *The Language of War*. Cambridge, MA: Harvard University Press, 2002.

Deleuze, Gilles. *Difference and Repetition*. Trans. Paul Patton. New York: Columbia University Press, 1994.

———. (with Félix Guattari.) *Kafka: Toward a Minor Literature*. Minneapolis: University of Minnesota Press, 1986.

———. *Proust and Signs: The Complete Text*. Trans. Richard Howard. Minneapolis: University of Minnesota Press, 2000.

de Man, Paul. *Blindness and Insight*. New York: Oxford University Press, 1971.

Descombes, Vincent. *Modern French Philosophy*. Trans. L. Scott-Fox and J. M. Harding. Cambridge: Cambridge University Press, 1980.

Dostoyevsky, Fyodor. *The Idiot*. Trans. and intro. David Magarshack. New York: Penguin Books, 1981.

Due, Reidar. *Deleuze*. Cambridge: Polity Press, 2007.

Eagleton, Terry. *Walter Benjamin, or Towards a Revolutionary Criticism.* London: Verso Books, 1981.

Ellman, Richard. *James Joyce*. New York: Oxford University Press, 1959.

Fitzgerald, Scott. *The Crack Up*. Ed. Edmund Wilson. New York: New Directions, 1954.

Foucault, Michel. *The Archaeology of Knowledge*. New York: Pantheon Books, 1972.

———. *Essential Works of Michel Foucault: Power*. Volume Three. Ed. James D. Faubion. Trans. Robert Hurley and others. New York: New Press, 2000.

———. *Language, Counter-memory, Practice: Selected Essays and Interviews by Michel Foucault*. Ed. Donald F. Bouchard. Trans. Donald F. Bouchard and Sherry Simon. Ithaca, NY: Cornell University Press, 1977.

———. *Michel Foucault: Politics, Philosophy, Culture: Interviews and Other Writings. 1977–1984*. Ed. Lawrence D. Kritzman. New York: Routledge, 1988.

———. *The Order of Things: An Archaeology of the Human Sciences*. New York: Pantheon Books, 1970.

Fry, Paul H. "The Image of Walter Benjamin." *Raritan* II, no. 4 (Spring, 1983).

Geismar, Maxwell. *Writers in Crisis: The American Novel, 1925–1940*. New York: Houghton Mifflin, 1942.

Gilman, Richard. *Decadence: The Strange Life of an Epithet*. New York: Farrar, Strauss and Giroux, 1980.

Hemingway, Gregory. *Papa: A Personal Memoir*. Houghton Mifflin, 1976.

Kuckl, John, and Jackson Bryer. *Dear Scott/Dear Max: The Fitzgerald-Perkins Correspondences*. New York: Scribner's, 1971.

Lajoie, Ronald, and Sally Lentz. "Is Jake Waiting?" *Fitzgerald/Hemingway Annual*, 1975.

Lynn, Kenneth, S. *Hemingway*. Cambridge, MA: Harvard University Press, 1987.

Meyers, Jeffrey, ed. *Hemingway: The Critical Heritage*. London: Routledge, 1982.

Nietzsche, Friedrich. *The Gay Science*. Trans. Walter Kaufmann. New York: Vintage Books, 1974.

Peckham, Morse. "Ernest Hemingway: Sexual Themes in His Writing." *Romanticism and Behavior*. Columbia: University of South Carolina Press, 1976.

Proust, Marcel. "Time Regained." *In Search of Lost Time*. Trans. Andreas Mayor and Terrence Kilmartin. Rev. D. J. Enright. New York: Modern Library, 2003.

Racevskis, Karlis. *Postmodernism and the Search for Enlightenment.* Charlottesville: University Press of Virginia, 1993.

Rajchman, John. *Michel Foucault: The Freedom of Philosophy.* New York: Columbia University Press, 1985.

Reynolds, Michael. *Hemingway's First War: The Making of* A Farewell to Arms. Princeton, NJ: Princeton University Press, 1976.

Rovit, Earl. *Ernest Hemingway.* Boston: G. K. Hall, 1963.

Said, Edward. *Beginnings: Intention and Method.* Baltimore: Johns Hopkins University Press, 1975.

———. "Secular Criticism." *Raritan* II, no. 3 (Winter, 1983).

Taylor, Ronald, and Ernst Block. *Aesthetics and Politics.* London: NLB, 1977.

Waldorn, Arthur. *A Reader's Guide to Ernest Hemingway.* New York: Octagon Books, 1981.

Wilson, Edmund. *To the Finland Station.* Garden City, NY: Doubleday, 1940.

———. *The Wound and the Bow: Seven Studies in Literature.* Cambridge, MA: Riverside Press, 1941.

Young, Philip. *Ernest Hemingway.* New York: Rinehart, 1952.

# Index

modernism in, 22
"necessary measures," 50–51
Paris as setting for, 37, 160
showing Hemingway's dissatisfaction with Paris, 55
portrait of Gertrude Stein in, 39,
50, 56, 158
"professionalism" in, 54
sexuality in, 50, 175
eroticism, 44
showing hunger for writing, 42
writers and writing in, 42
"My Old Man" in *In Our Time* (Hemingway), 180
"myth" of Hemingway, 116, 122, 127,
175

naivety of Hemingway, 26
NANA. *See* North American News-
paper Alliance
"Natural History of the Dead, A"
(Hemingway), 72, 79, 80–85, 90.
*See also Death in the Afternoon*
(Hemingway)
naturalist, Hemingway as a, 144, 167
in "Big Two Hearted River,"
39–40
in *Death in the Afternoon*, 111
in *Green Hills of Africa*, 99,
100–101, 107, 109
"necessary measures," 50
*Negotiations* (Deleuze), 188
*New Masses*, 94
*New Science* (Vico), 191
*New Yorker*, 94
Nicanor, John Hadley. *See* Hemingway,
John "Jack" Hadley Nicanor
Nietzsche, Friedrich, 85, 93, 96, 106,
120, 133, 167, 188
"Nietzsche, Genealogy, History" (Fou-
cault), 189–90

nihilism, 63, 70, 85, 141, 187
Nobel Prize, 29, 148, 185
North American Newspaper Alliance,
125
nostalgia, debilitating force of, 89–90
*Notes from the Underground* (Dostoyevsky), 141
novels, Hemingway's experiments with,
63

obsession, writing as an, 11, 18, 33,
48, 106, 115, 144, 148, 185
O'Hara, John, 19
old age and youthfulness as themes in
Hemingway's last works
in *Across the River and Into the
Trees*, 150, 157
in *A Farewell to Arms*, 61
in *The Old Man and the Sea*, 150,
157, 162
*Old Man and the Sea, The* (Hemingway), 148–49, 157–59, 160–67, 185
artists as theme in, 169
as a counter-concept to decadence,
166–67
courage in, 158
critical reception of, 56, 148
death in, 166
detachment in, 162
education in, 150
fishing in, 149, 150, 158, 160–61,
162, 163–64, 165–66, 185
*la mar* in, 160, 161, 162, 164
as a late work of Hemingway, 27,
148, 150, 161
old age and youthfulness, 150,
157
public reception of, 158–59
simplicity, Hemingway's use of in,
161
"Old Man at the Bridge" in *The First*